True Peace and Security

and Security

—FROM WHAT SOURCE?

Is there a real solution to the problems that mankind now faces? This book is published with the conviction that there is. It is our sincere desire that by reading it you will gain a solid hope and a heartwarming assurance as to what the future holds for all who truly love righteousness.

—The Publishers

C☉NTENTS

The scriptures referred to in this book may be found in any translation of the Bible. However, unless otherwise indicated, direct quotations are from the modern-language *New World Translation of the Holy Scriptures,* 1971 edition. Listed below are the abbreviations of names of other Bible versions quoted:

Dy – Roman Catholic *Douay Version,* of 1610.
NE – *The New English Bible,* of 1970.
Ro – *The Emphasised Bible,* of 1897, Joseph B. Rotherham.

CHAPTER 1

The Choice We All Face

SURELY you, like most persons today, want peace and security. People everywhere are weary of war, tension and turmoil. They long for relief. Would you not rejoice to see this earth become a pleasant, secure home for all of its inhabitants?

² There is every reason to believe that the longed-for relief is now at hand! From what source?

³ World leaders today are confidently foretelling the entry of a 'new era' in world history. They say that the threat of global war and nuclear destruction is past. Why? Because, they declare, a dramatic change in relations between the world's great powers is bringing in a time of peace and security such as the world has never seen. In January of 1973 a prominent statesman said: "We have made a breakthrough toward creating in the world what the world has not known before—a structure of peace that can last, not merely for our time, but for generations to come."[1]

⁴ The question is: What is required in order to make the peace and security *genuine?* How can it make *your* life secure? To accomplish that, would it not have to reach into your neighborhood and your home and solve the problems that seriously affect you? Would it not also have to

---

1-4. (a) What conditions have you seen that make you realize how desirable it would be to have true peace and security? (b) On what basis are world leaders foretelling that they expect lasting peace? (c) If any arrangement for peace and security is to benefit your own life, what kind of problems must it solve?

solve the problems of growing crime and drug addiction, rising food çosts and heavy taxation, spreading pollution and the steady weakening of family ties? Surely, as long as any of these situations continue, they are a threat to your personal peace and security.

⁵ Men today offer the hope that they can over-come the major problems afflicting mankind. They say that, freed from the crushing burdens of war, they can direct wealth, research and manpower far more energetically toward finding remedies for such things as crime, disease, hunger, poverty and bad housing.

⁶ Do you believe this? Is there any solid evidence from the past or from the present to show that men are able to bring such solutions? What does human history show? What does your own experience in life tell you?

⁷ 'But if men do not have the solution, what remains?' you may ask. 'What choice do we have?' Well, what about God? There is the undeniable fact that the earth and the living things on it give evidence of intelligent design. (Hebrews 3:4) So, then, where does God enter the picture? Is he concerned? Will he take a hand in human affairs?

⁸ In view of what is at stake, is it not worth your while to examine what the Bible says on this matter? You may realize that the Bible is the most widely translated* and circulated book on earth. But did you know that it discusses the very

---

* Now in 1,500 languages and dialects.

5-8. (a) On the basis of your own experience in life, do you be-lieve that men are going to solve those problems? (b) Where else might we look for a solution? (c) How prominent a book is the Bible?

matters that are of greatest concern to us in this twentieth century?

[9] Many people have heard that it foretells a coming world destruction, and this may disturb them. But few know what it says as to when that destruction will come or about its prophecies of life right here on earth afterward. (Matthew 24:21, 22; 2 Peter 3:11-13) They may have prayed for 'God's kingdom to come.' But few realize that the Bible speaks of that kingdom as an actual government, one that will shortly replace all present political systems.—Daniel 2:44.

[10] There is a vast difference between the peace and security the Bible shows that God's kingdom will bring and what human leaders of our day promise. Today men speak in terms of a reduction of arms by treaties and peace pacts. The Bible, by contrast, says that soon God will bring a complete end to all armaments and remove the root causes of war. The security that God promises is not just from war between nations. It is from enemies of any kind, anywhere, so that no one need be in fear, day or night. (Micah 4:3, 4) Men are now concerned with bringing crime under control, but God's declared purpose is to wipe out even the sources of crime, rooting out the attitudes and conditions with which crime begins. (Psalm 37:8-11 [36:8-11, Catholic *Douay Version*]; Galatians 5:19-21) The nations speak of progress in medical research and improved care of the sick and aged. But the Bible explains how God's government will bring about full and lasting

---

9. What does the Bible say about the future of mankind and of government?

10. What are some of the differences between what the Bible says that God's kingdom will do and what human leaders say that they will do?

health, yes, even overcoming the problems of aging and death. (Revelation 21:3, 4) Under the kind of rulership described in the Bible, a person's work will mean more than just getting money or possessions—it will make life meaningful, filled with purpose, bringing real satisfaction. For, after all, no matter what you are paid, how happy can you be if your work is monotonous, if you feel frustrated and without a true sense of accomplishment in life?—Romans 8:19-21; Isaiah 65:21-23.

[11] Which would you prefer? Which do you believe offers true peace and security? By going along with what the world in general accepts, have you really found what you want in life? If you let yourself be carried along with what may currently be popular, may you find that you have trusted in a false peace, a fraudulent security that leaves you, not only disillusioned, but also in grave danger? On the other hand, can you rely on what the Bible promises as something believable, practical, realistic?

[12] The choice we each face is not one of minor consequence. Our very lives are at stake. Surely, then, the answer to the questions raised deserves your thoughtful examination.

---

11. In deciding whether to put our trust in men or in what the Bible promises, what questions do we do well to ask ourselves?
12. Why would it be beneficial for us to examine together the answers to these questions?

CHAPTER 2

Can Men Bring Lasting Peace
and Security?

GENUINE hope is founded on reality and truth.
False hopes only blind people to the true
hope, deceiving them. In a time of crisis such as
we now face, false hopes would even rob a person
of his life.

² Therefore, we need to ask ourselves: Do we
clearly appreciate just how big the problems are
that must be solved to bring genuine peace and
security? Do we realize how urgent the situation
has become? What evidence do we actually have
that men's solutions would be equal to the im-
mensity of the task?

³ Also, we face the question of whether we can
put our trust in world leaders and in God at the
same time. Some believe that they can. They
believe that current human efforts toward
bringing lasting peace have God's backing. But
do they? Since so much lies in the balance, we do
well to examine the facts.

URGENCY AND FEAR MOVE MEN TO ACTION

⁴ For thousands of years men have sought
lasting peace and security, without success. But

1. Why is it important that our hope for peace and security be
based on reality and truth?
2, 3. (a) What questions would it be beneficial to ask ourselves
as to the problems involved in bringing peace and security?
(b) What further question faces those who claim to have faith
in God?
4-6. To what realization have world leaders come as to the serious-
ness of the problems facing mankind?

now there is a new circumstance that many believe will cause men to come to grips with the problems and to succeed. What is this new circumstance?

⁵ It is that, for the first time, world leaders are acknowledging that they must decide between world peace and world suicide. They agree that an all-out nuclear war would be so deadly that there could be no winners, only losers. Not only this, but many, especially scientists, say that there is even greater danger from worldwide pollution, and also from the "population explosion," with the widespread famine, disease and unrest that this threatens to bring. They say that time is running out for global action by all nations if worldwide disaster is to be avoided. As a report from Washington, D.C., states:

"Suddenly in any number of disparate countries— the United States, Britain, France, Germany, Italy, Sweden, Czechoslovakia, the Soviet Union, India, Japan—influential men have sensed an impending danger unlike any in human experience. Futurologists call it the crisis of crises, the culmination of man's timeless errors."—Washington *Post*.[2]

⁶ These men recognize that, even though mankind might survive these crises one at a time, they could not survive *if all, or even several of them, hit at once*. The question is, however, Will fear of disaster really turn mankind away from disunity and strife to a course bringing true peace and security?

A WARLESS WORLD BY MEN'S EFFORTS?

⁷ What real reason does any of us have to be-

7-11. (a) As to man's ability to put an end to war, what does history show? (b) Is fear of atomic warfare a sound foundation for peace? (c) Does the signing of disarmament pacts or peace treaties guarantee lasting peace?

lieve that men can bring a complete end to war?
What does history show?

[8] True, there have been a few scattered years
when this planet Earth was free from war. But
very few. Military analyst Hanson W. Baldwin
calculated that in some 3,457 years of recorded
history, there have been more than 3,230 years
of war and only 227 years of peace.[3]

[9] But will not the mutual fear of atomic warfare
change this? Remember, men learned to fear
nuclear weapons over a quarter of a century ago,
when atomic bombs wiped out two Japanese
cities. But what has their fear moved them to do
since then? Actually, it has led them to stockpile
more and more such weapons and even to keep
inventing others of vastly greater destructive
power.

[10] Do you not agree that, instead of ensuring
true peace, fear produced by threat of attack in
reality creates suspicion and tension? If you keep
peace with your neighbor only because you know
he is armed and threatens to use his weapons, is
this real peace? Can you ever feel secure while
that neighbor lives alongside you? Actually, such
fear can easily lead to hasty, thoughtless, violent
acts. Surely the "balance of terror" that world
leaders have built up is no foundation for genuine
peace.

[11] Granted, the nations may sign disarmament
pacts or peace treaties. But over the centuries
literally thousands of these have been signed.
Yet, whenever war sentiment became strong
enough, those treaties proved worthless, mere
scraps of paper. Is it realistic to think that world
leaders today will keep their word if selfish
nationalistic interests seem to dictate otherwise?

More importantly, will you risk your hope of life in peace and security on their promise to keep peace?

[12] What, then, about the Bible? Does it urge us to put our hope and confidence in human efforts to bring peace, in the face of all the evidence showing man's inability to achieve it? To the contrary, it foretold long ago that, by themselves, men would never bring lasting peace. It forewarned that, even during the period just before God's kingdom would clean out of the earth all who do not have true love for righteousness, there would be "wars and disorders," with 'nation rising against nation and kingdom against kingdom' in global warfare. (Luke 21:9, 10, 31; Revelation 6:1-4) The greatest, most destructive slaughter in human history has taken place in our generation in two world wars. And since the end of World War II there have been over three hundred wars or violent uprisings, an average of about one a month! *What the Bible foretold is consistent with what has actually occurred.* It gave us no false hope.

[13] The Bible also identifies the real source of the problem. It shows that war is not caused by bullets or bombs or battleships but by *people,* by human selfishness. (James 4:1-3) If men are to achieve lasting peace, they must first bring about a worldwide change in people. But on the basis of man's record over the centuries, would you say that such a thing is likely? What about the record of *this* generation? Does it indicate that such a change is impending—that people

---

12, 13. (a) How has what the Bible foretold about man's failure to achieve lasting peace been consistent with what has occurred? (b) What does the Bible identify as the real source of war?

everywhere are abandoning their selfishness, their divisive nationalism, their racial hatred, their commercial greed? Certainly not! And the Bible truthfully states that, when men seek peace only so that they can continue their pursuit of selfishness, they will never succeed.—Isaiah 57:19-21; 59:7, 8.

CAN MEN KEEP THE "HUMAN BOMB" FROM EXPLODING?

[14] Earth's population reached one billion (one thousand million) persons for the first time early in the nineteenth century. By 1930 it grew to two billion. There are now over 3.6 billion persons on earth, and estimates are that the figure will pass six billion in the next thirty years! What does this mean?

[15] It means that every day there are some 200,000 more mouths to be fed. And most of these are in areas where poverty, hunger and disease already affect millions. As food science professor Georg Borgstrom, of Michigan State University, said:

"Anyone who thinks that the current world protein crisis is going to blow over and take care of itself should remember: the hungry of the world are multiplying twice at fast as the well fed."[4]

[16] But have not agricultural scientists developed new high-yield strains of rice, wheat and corn in what has been hailed as a "green revolution"? Yes, but will this answer the world's hunger problem? More and more food experts now say, No. Many warn that the new varieties of grains

14-17. (a) How rapidly is the earth's population increasing, and what does this mean as to the problem of providing food? (b) As to whether scientists have the needed solution, what do they themselves say?

may even contribute to famine. How? A 1971 Associated Press dispatch reported:

> "The new hybrids are not as blight-resistant as the older types. There is the possibility that a country's entire crop—perhaps a world crop—would be wiped out by a new plant disease. It almost happened last year with the corn crop in the United States."[5]

[17] It is, in fact, the scientists themselves who most frequently warn that they do not have the solution. As one prominent biologist expressed it:

> "Some feel that the battle to feed the world population is now lost, and that it is a foregone conclusion that by 1985 we will have world-wide famines in which hundreds of millions of people will starve to death. I must admit that at this time I see no major crash program which would lead me to disagree with this conclusion."[6]

[18] With all its agricultural science, modern society has not been able to avoid the very conditions of which the Bible forewarned. It accurately foretold the arrival of severe food shortages on a worldwide scale during the "conclusion of the system of things."—Matthew 24:3, 7; Revelation 6:5-8.

[19] Much of the problem lies, not with agricultural methods primarily, but with people and their attitudes that go contrary to Bible principles. For decades now, the nations have spent vast sums on armaments while millions earth wide face starvation. According to a United Nations report, in recent years the nations have been spending $200 billion a year on their armed forces. That is more than the total annual income of a third of the earth's population!

18-21. (a) What did the Bible foretell about this situation? (b) Would cutting back the amount of military spending solve the problem? (c) Why has such a serious situation developed?

²⁰ Even if the enormous military buildup were abandoned, the world's divided economic system works against any true relief for the problem. Even when food is available, desire for big profits often prevents its distribution to those in need. In some lands, governments pay farmers not to produce certain crops and, rather than let high production bring a decrease in price, crops are even destroyed.

²¹ How different all this is from the principles set forth in the Bible encouraging a loving attitude toward those in need. (Deuteronomy 24:19-21) Men have built up their economic systems on selfishness and, rather than bringing peace and security, a situation that threatens disastrous consequences has now developed. Sooner or later men 'reap what they sow,' even as the Bible points out.—Galatians 6:7.

CAN MEN MAKE PEACE WITH THE EARTH?

²² For scores of years now, men have been making war with the very earth on which they live. How? By worldwide pollution. Pollution is poisonous waste that man has caused and that has backed up into his water supply, into the air he breathes and the food he eats, until he cannot push it away. Thus man has endangered the most basic elements he needs for life.

²³ Those trusting in men to bring peace and security say that man will find a way to survive this crisis as he has survived past crises. They believe that human science will provide the solution.

22-25. (a) How serious is the problem of pollution? (b) Though some persons look to human science to provide the solution, what do the scientists say?

²⁴ But, once more, the ones expressing the gravest doubts today are the scientists themselves. Note the following:

"Dr. William D. McElroy, outgoing director of the National Science Foundation, said recently that a natural reaction to the threat posed by pollution is that man has survived other dangers before and can do it again. This, unfortunately, 'is not at all in accord with the facts. The simple truth today is that man's survival in an acceptable society is by no means assured . . . Self-destruction by environmental degradation is a real possibility.' "—Atlanta *Journal*.[7]

²⁵ Men can invent and mass-produce machines, creating an industrialized society. But in using the machines, they are ruining their own environment. As Dr. René Dubos, a pollution authority, says:

"In my opinion, there is no chance of solving the problem of pollution—or the other threats to human life—if we accept the idea that technology is to rule our future."[8]

²⁶ Again, the Bible foretold man's lack of wisdom in his use of earth's bounties. The prophecy at Revelation 11:18 foretold the time when God would have to take action "to bring to ruin those ruining the earth."

²⁷ And, once more, it becomes evident that the Bible reliably focuses on the true source of mankind's pollution problems. Is it industry and machines? Not primarily. Primarily it is *people* who cause pollution. They pollute because of selfish desire or ignorance or both. They have built up the present economic systems to fulfill

26-28. (a) Did the Bible foretell that such a critical situation would develop in regard to the earth? (b) What really is the source of the pollution problem? (c) In coping with the problems of pollution, what vital knowledge do human scientists lack, but who has it?

their desires, but now they find these systems taking away the very things they need in order to enjoy life.

28 True, there is much said today about ecology and research into earth's environment. But scientists still do not understand fully how earth's "ecosystems" (the biological relationships on which life depends) work. *Time* magazine says of these ecosystems:

> "Even the simplest is so complex that the largest computer cannot fully unravel it."[9]

Men admittedly do not understand the complex ecology of earth. But God does, because he created it. Is it not wise and practical to look to the Creator of these things to provide the solution to the problems?

SECURITY BY THE REMOVAL OF CRIME

29 Though pollution endangers the very essentials for human existence, it is the increase of crime that causes the greater number of people to be in fear. Crime steadily is robbing more and more persons of their personal security, not only in big cities, but in small towns and rural areas. Not just possessions but often one's own body is in jeopardy. Can men bring you true security from these dangers?

30 Can they do it by new legislation? There are already hundreds, even thousands, of laws on the lawbooks of the world. Yet, these have not stopped the rise in crime. Also, deep-rooted corruption often develops right within the law-enforcement bodies themselves. Dishonesty in high places may

---

29-31. (a) How widespread is the problem of crime? (b) Why would not the passing of new laws eliminate crime? (c) What indicates that material prosperity would not solve the problem?

nullify the efforts of law-enforcement officers who are honest. And the fact remains that righteousness cannot be injected into people's hearts by laws.

[31] Does the answer lie in new methods of detecting and thwarting crime? For every new method produced, criminals devise new ways to overcome it. Then, will increased prosperity in a man-made "era of peace" solve the problem? It would certainly be a mistake to conclude that crime is characteristic only of lower-income groups. For example, note this report:

> "The number of crimes committed by business and professional men in Australia had risen to a startling degree in the past two or three years."—*The Australian*.[10]

Also, the New York *Times* reports that theft in the Wall Street financial district is like a "free-for-all," adding: "Everybody is stealing—the messengers, the clerks, even the supervisory personnel."[11] The facts show that the highest crime rates are found in the wealthier industrial nations. And not to be overlooked is the rising tide of drug addiction.

[32] What is happening is as Bible prophecies long ago foretold: "In the last days critical times hard to deal with will be here. For men will be lovers of themselves, . . . without self-control, fierce, without love of goodness, . . . lovers of pleasures rather than lovers of God." (2 Timothy 3:1-4) Particularly noteworthy is that these conditions were prophesied to exist among persons *claiming* to have faith in God, but proving false to their claim. (Verse 5) And do we not find that today

---

32. Has what the Bible foretold about this situation been fulfilled?

the nations of Christendom are those hardest hit by crime and similar social ills? Jesus also foretold an "increasing of lawlessness" for the period just before God's kingdom would destroy the wicked to make the earth a place to be 'inherited by mild-tempered persons.' That "increasing of lawlessness" is a fact of life in our day. —Matthew 24:12; 5:5.

THE GREATEST PROBLEMS OF ALL

[33] Suppose men could solve the problems of war, poverty, hunger, pollution, crime and drug addiction. Would this bring you full peace and security? No, something would still be lacking. Sickness and death still remain as unconquered enemies of your security. Indeed, what would peace from all other problems mean or matter if one had to watch a loved member of his family sicken and die, or find his own body attacked by a fatal illness?

[34] Impressive medical advances have been made in recent times. But what real security does this bring us? What do medical authorities themselves recognize?

[35] A report in the *Wall Street Journal*,[12] under the headline "Science Loses Ground in War Against Disease in Impoverished Lands," shows that three diseases (malaria, trachoma, schistosomiasis) now afflict 800 million people in such nations. And medical reports indicate that the number affected is growing steadily. So almost one fourth of the world's population is plagued by just three of many diseases.

33-38. (a) Even if men could solve all the problems discussed thus far, what greater enemies of peace and security would still remain? (b) What prospects do medical researchers see for conquering the major diseases that afflict mankind?

³⁶ What of the more wealthy nations? Here heart disease is the number one killer. At a recent Conference on Hunger and Malnutrition, heart disease was called an "epidemic." In Canada it afflicts one out of four adults. In the United States over 50 percent of the deaths each year are from heart disease, with many younger men now among the victims. Yet, according to a report in the New York *Times,* "Dr. Moses, the American Heart Association official, said that physicians recognize that they cannot 'stamp out' heart disease."¹³

³⁷ The number of victims from the dreaded disease of cancer also keeps growing. What hope of relief? Columbia University Professor of Surgeons Harry Grundfest states: "There are only vague clues as yet as to the nature of the cancer problem—let alone its solution."¹⁴

³⁸ Even the most enthusiastic men in medical science admit that in our lifetime it is unlikely that cures will be found for heart disease, cancer, malaria and the other most deadly diseases. Even if they did, they realize that this would still do little to lengthen the average life-span of most persons. People would still get old and die. So, then, what real hope of security from disease, aging and death can men offer?

³⁹ Though written thousands of years ago, how true the words in the Bible at Job 14:1, 2 continue to be today: "Man, born of woman, is short-lived and glutted with agitation. Like a blossom he has come forth and is cut off, and he runs away like the shadow and does not keep existing." The Bible also shows the reason for this, and it identi-

─────────────────────────

39. Where can we learn the reason why human life is so short and filled with problems?

fies the primary, unseen cause of all man's problems, as we shall see later.

IN WHAT WILL YOU HOPE?

40 In all honesty, then, is it realistic to trust in world leaders or other men to solve the problems facing mankind? Or is it more realistic to put trust in the solution to which the Bible points, namely, action by God himself through a righteous heavenly government? Long ago the inspired psalmist wrote these words:

"Do not put your trust in nobles, nor in the son of earthling man, to whom no salvation belongs. His spirit goes out, he goes back to his ground; in that day his thoughts do perish. Happy is the one who has the God of Jacob for his help, whose hope is in Jehovah his God, the Maker of heaven and earth, of the sea, and of all that is in them."—Psalm 146:3-6 [145:2-6, *Dy*].

41 Never forget that, no matter how sincere men may be or how influential and powerful they may be as world leaders, they are all dying creatures. Unable to save themselves, how can they save others?

40, 41. Which do you believe—that it is more realistic to look to men to solve the problems facing mankind, or that only God can do this? Why?

CHAPTER 3

Are the World's Religions Giving the Right Lead?

WHATEVER your attitude toward religion, you surely recognize the great influence it has had upon mankind. As the 1970 *World Book Encyclopedia* states: "Religion has been one of the most powerful forces in history."[15]

2 With all their influence over hundreds of millions of persons, are the world's religions a genuine force for peace and security? Or have they contributed to the turmoil on the earth? Could it be that they actually bear the greatest responsibility for bringing mankind face-to-face with world destruction?

3 These questions may sound startling. But we may remember that Christ Jesus said of religious leaders of his day: "Let them be. Blind guides is what they are. If, then, a blind man guides a blind man, both will fall into a pit." (Matthew 15:14) Today, there are hundreds of religions claiming to be Christian and these boast of nearly a billion members. The nations of Christendom are among the most powerful in the world. Surely what the religions of Christendom have taught has had much to do with world conditions. So, then, do they live up to their claim to represent God and Christ Jesus and to follow the Bible as God's Word? Or is it possible that they, as well as the world's other religions, in reality are lead-

1-3. (a) What important questions regarding the world's religions are here raised? (b) Why are these questions appropriate?

ing mankind into conflict with God, a conflict that can bring only disaster?

⁴ If you seek peaceful, secure living for yourself and your family, you should welcome a frank consideration of these questions. The answer to them will also reveal something else to you. It will enable you to know just how reliable the Bible is, the strength of its claim to being the Word of God. Why?

⁵ Because the Bible says there is both true religion and false. And it states that God approves and blesses only worship that is founded on truth, free from hypocrisy and deceit. (Matthew 15:7-9; John 4:23, 24; Titus 1:16) It declares that only true worship in full harmony with God's Word can produce people who live in peace and unity, with genuine love for one another. (Isaiah 32:17, 18; John 13:35) If this is the case, then certainly religion that goes contrary to the Bible could never succeed in leading mankind to true peace and security. Has this been the case?

WHAT LEAD DOES WORLD RELIGION GIVE AS TO WAR?

⁶ The Bible refers to God as the one "who gives peace." (Romans 16:20) And his people are instructed to "seek peace and pursue it," to "beat their swords into plowshares" and not to learn war anymore. (1 Peter 3:11; Isaiah 2:2-4) Such peace earth wide can come only if people first 'love their neighbors as themselves.'—Matthew 22:39.

4, 5. In what way can the answers to these questions help us to find out how reliable the Bible is?
6. Before there can be true peace, what must people do?

⁷ Have this world's religions taught their followers such love? Have they taught them that this love should surmount national boundaries and racial or language differences? Have the churches of Christendom, Catholic and Protestant, proved true to their claim to follow Jesus Christ as "the Prince of Peace"? Though it may surprise many, history proves that the opposite is true.

⁸ As the New York *Times* observed: "In the past local Catholic hierarchies almost always supported the wars of their nations, blessing troops and offering prayers for victory, while another group of [Catholic] bishops on the other side publicly prayed for the opposite outcome."¹⁶ Protestant religious leaders did the same.

⁹ Typical was World War I, which broke out in the heart of Christendom. The vast majority of men on both sides were of the same religions. The Belgian newspaper *La Dernière Heure* relates that during the war Roman Catholic Cardinal Amette of Paris said this to the French soldiers:

> "My brothers, comrades of the French army and of their glorious allies, the Almighty God is on our side. . . . God is near to our brave soldiers in battle, he gives them strength and fortifies them against the enemy. . . . God will give us the victory."¹⁷

¹⁰ At the same time, on the other side, the Catholic archbishop of Cologne, Germany, said to German soldiers:

> "God is with us in this fight for righteousness . . . We command you in the name of God, to fight to the last drop of your blood for the honor and glory of the country. . . . God knows that we are

7-12. What do the facts show as to whether the world's religions have taught the kind of love that would promote international peace?

on the side of righteousness and he will give us the victory."[17]

[11] Do the churches represent God when they give such contradictory, hate-filled leadership? After Italy invaded Ethiopia in 1935, the Pittsburgh *Courier* commented:

"The church follows the flag, even though the flag be drenched with the blood of innocent victims of war madness slaughtered in the name of civilization . . .

"And just as the Catholic Church has either approved or seldom disapproved of this international robbery, exploitation and murder, so have the Protestant churches. . . .

"In large part, the spiritual weakness of the Christian Church today is ascribable to its constant compromise with the evils it is supposed to combat."[18]

[12] During World War II and in wars since then, the churches followed the same pat-

BAN THE BOMB? THE CHURCH SAYS "NO!"

CAN Christians use the atom bomb? And is economic planning, which tries to ensure that the means of life are shared more equally and in greater abundance by . . .

FORWARD, May 31, 1947

Catholics and Viet-Nam

Ramparts Magazine Says Cardinal Spellman And Others Helped Push U.S. Into Viet-Nam

By Drew Pearson

THE WASHINGTON POST Sunday, July 4, 1965

Adventist Youth Prepared for War Front Service

ADVENTIST, February 15, 1951

TIME, JULY 13, 1970

NORTHERN IRELAND

Another 'Guerrilla' Priest

By R. S. COCHRANE

Panama American, March 5, 1970

Nazi Army Praised

German Catholic Bishops Loyal

BERLIN, Aug. 27 (AP)—A solemn pledge of loyalty to Hitler by the German Catholic bishops conference at Fulda is to be read to the faithful from pul-

NEW YORK POST, 1940

METHODISTS INDORSE WAR WITH GERMANY

Assert Peace at Any Price Is Too Dearly Bought—Urge Prohibition as a War Measure.

NEW YORK TIMES, 1917

Lutherans Promise Support, Even to War, Of U.S. Steps in Crisis

By Caspar Nannes
Star Staff Correspondent

MILWAUKEE, June 28—The Lutheran Church-Missouri Synod in an unusual action today issued a declaration pledging the denomination's support . . .

STAR, 1950

Did you know that the churches were so deeply involved in war?

tern. What, then, of the religions outside Christendom? Is their record different? To the contrary, members of the same non-Christian religions have often killed one another in violent strife and warfare, as history abundantly testifies. Often their religious teachings uphold such violence and bloodshed.

[13] True, in times of peace religious leaders praise peace; then it is popular to do so. And you may at times hear or read of those who take a stand against war even when such a stand is not popular. Yet these same religious leaders frequently show they are not genuinely peaceful, for they engage in protest actions that are often violent. Some even advocate sabotage and revolt against existing governments. But the Bible condemns such a course.—Romans 12:17-19; 13:1, 2.

[14] The influence of the world's religions over the nations of earth has been so great that the Bible describes these religions collectively as an *empire*. They are spoken of under the name "Babylon the Great," which is said to be "the great city that has a kingdom over the kings of the earth." (Revelation 17:3-5, 15, 18) Because the world's religions have undeniably 'prostituted' themselves for political and commercial and social gain, this religious empire, Babylon the Great, is pictured as a "harlot." Of this harlotrous religious empire it is said: "In her was found the blood of . . . all those who have been slaughtered on the earth." (Revelation 18:24) Does that sound shocking—that the world's religions bear

---

13. Does the Bible agree with the actions of those clergymen who, in the name of peace, engage in violent protest against existing governments?
14. (a) In what symbolic language are the world's religions described in the Bible? (b) What guilt is charged against "Babylon the Great"?

the principal guilt for all the slaughter of world history? Yet the influence they wield and the lead they have set in supporting war, as well as carrying on violent crusades and religious persecution, bring exactly that responsibility upon them.—Compare Matthew 23:33-36; 27:20-23, 25.

¹⁵ The Bible's teaching is "that we should have love for one another; not like Cain, who originated with the wicked one [Satan the Devil] and slaughtered his brother." (1 John 3:10-12) Yet mankind continues in the course of Cain, and the world's religions have blessed those pursuing that course. If you are a church member, ask yourself, 'What about my own religion? If all persons belonged to my religion, would wars have stopped and this earth now be a place of genuine peace?'

DO THE WORLD'S RELIGIONS
PROMOTE MORALITY?

¹⁶ Can anyone enjoy true peace with his neighbors or real security if there is no holding to true standards of morality? Obviously not. Without this there will be lying, stealing, adultery, and similar practices. Genuine love of neighbor should promote morality. As the Bible expresses it:

"He that loves his fellowman has fulfilled the law. For the law code, 'You must not commit adultery, You must not murder, You must not steal, You must not covet,' and whatever other commandment there is, is summed up in this word, namely, 'You must love your neighbor as yourself.' Love does

15. If persons who are church members really want peace, what questions must they be willing to face as to their own church?
16. (a) Why is the holding to true standards of morality an important factor in peace and security? (b) As taught in the Bible, what promotes such morality?

not work evil to one's neighbor; therefore love is the law's fulfillment."—Romans 13:8-10.

[17] More important than this, however, do you believe that anyone can be at peace with God, having the assurance of His favor and protection, if he does not practice true morality? Could you respect and honor God if he did not require such morality from those whom he approves?

[18] Surely for God to require righteousness he would have to make clear to his creatures what his moral standards are. To say that each person should make up his own standards and go by them would be no more reasonable than to say that each person should make up his own traffic laws and go by them. You know what the result would be. The Bible logically shows that there is only one way bringing God's approval and that any other road leads only to destruction. —Matthew 7:13, 14.

[19] Well, do Christendom's churches truthfully represent the Bible, upholding its standards of morality and so setting a lead for the rest of the world? What do the lives of those who belong to these churches show? The Bible says that the "fruitage of [God's] spirit is love, joy, peace, long-suffering, kindness, goodness, faith, mildness, self-control." (Galatians 5:22, 23) Is *this* the fruitage that the world's religions produce? Or do you find instead a surprising amount of "rotten" fruit, "the works of the flesh . . . fornication, uncleanness, loose conduct, idolatry, practice of spiritism, enmities, strife, jealousy, fits of anger, contentions, divisions, sects, envies,

17, 18. (a) Can we expect to enjoy peace with God if we do not hold to righteous moral standards? (b) Who sets those standards? 19. If Christendom's churches were setting a fine lead in morality, what would you expect to see in the lives of their members?

drunken bouts, revelries"? (Galatians 5:19-21) Likening men to trees, the Bible says that every "tree" producing such fruit is due to be destroyed. —Matthew 7:17-19; 12:33.

[20] If you belong to some religion, ask yourself: 'How confident and secure do I feel about the moral standards of its members? If all persons on earth lived like the members of my religion do, would that put an end to crime, dishonest business practices, strife and sexual immorality?'

[21] There is obvious truth in the Bible's warning that "a little leaven ferments the whole lump," and that "bad associations spoil useful habits." (Galatians 5:9; 1 Corinthians 15:33) That is why the inspired apostle wrote Christians: "Quit mixing in company with anyone called a brother that is a fornicator or a greedy person or an idolater or a reviler or a drunkard or an extortioner, not even eating with such a man. . . . 'Remove the wicked man from among yourselves.'"—1 Corinthians 5:11-13.

[22] True, a person may make a momentary misstep and then recover. But what of those of whom the apostle writes, those who *practice* such things, making them a part of their life? If such persons claim to be serving God, they are hypocrites. Surely you detest hypocrisy, and the Bible shows that God hates it and those who practice it. (Matthew 23:27, 28; Romans 12:9) What, then, of your religion? Do its religious leaders protect its members from spiritual danger by 'reproving before all onlookers persons who practice sin'? (1 Timothy 5:20) Do they clean out those who

---

20-22. (a) As to morality, what questions need to be asked about the members of one's own church? (b) What does the Bible say should be done about a congregation member who becomes a practicer of immorality? (c) Is this done in the churches?

Is this the kind of guidance that you want for your family?

persist in wrongdoing, showing no genuine repentance over it? Or do they allow such ones to remain as members in good standing, infecting others? Do they render mere 'lip service' to morality while actually condoning or 'winking' at wrongdoing?—Matthew 15:7, 8.

²³ Throughout the world, evidence mounts against the world's religions, evidence that they have not been a genuine force for morality and the security and peace it brings. More and more religious leaders today are saying publicly that fornication, adultery and homosexuality are not necessarily wrong. You yourself may have read news items to that effect. These represent the trend in the world's religions. But they do not represent the Bible, which says:

23. (a) What are many clergymen saying these days about such things as fornication, adultery and homosexuality? (b) What does the Bible say about such conduct?

"Do not be misled. Neither fornicators, nor idolaters, nor adulterers, nor men kept for unnatural purposes, nor men who lie with men, nor thieves, nor greedy persons, nor drunkards, nor revilers, nor extortioners will inherit God's kingdom."—1 Corinthians 6:9, 10.

[24] You may feel that the leaders of your religion are firm for moral standards. But have you ever personally asked your minister what his views are on these matters? You deserve to know and need to know, for your very hope of life is involved.

FREEDOM FROM GREED AND SELFISHNESS

[25] Greed and selfishness are clearly at the root of so much of today's strife and insecurity. The Bible says that the "love of money is a root of all sorts of injurious things." (1 Timothy 6:10) Are the world's religions, and particularly those of Christendom, free of this?

[26] Is it not true that the regular practice of churches in Christendom is to assess dues, exact tithes, pass the collection plate, promote fund-raising drives and ask publicly for money in religious radio and television programs or by mail? When church members desire the service of religious leaders, do they not generally feel obligated to pay—for example, for baptism, marriage or burial services? And throughout the world people who may be in real poverty are asked and pressured to finance the construction of costly cathedrals and temples.

[27] In many lands the world's religions have

24. How can a person find out for sure what the minister in his church believes about such conduct?
25. What effect does the "love of money" have on human relations?
26, 27. How have the world's religions shown their attitude toward money and the amassing of landholdings?

made a record of amassing wealth and huge land-holdings. In the nineteenth century, the Roman Catholic Church in Mexico owned not less than *one half of all the real estate in that land.*[19] Likewise in many lands with non-Christian religions, the greatest collection of wealth very often is in the religious temples, generally in stark contrast to the poverty of much of the population surrounding them.

[28] Contrast this with the teaching of Jesus Christ, who told his disciples: "You received free, give free." (Matthew 10:8) The Bible record shows that among the original Christians all giving was voluntary, without pressure. (Acts 11:29, 30; 2 Corinthians 9:7) Those taking the lead, apostles and others, were not a burden to their Christian brothers nor did they enrich themselves at their brothers' expense. They worked with their own hands. (Acts 18:1-4; 20:33-35) Is this true of religious leaders you know?

[29] Compare the world's religious leaders today with the religious leaders who opposed Jesus in the first century C.E. Though doing certain charitable works, those men loved glory and prominence and cultivated the favor of political leaders. (Matthew 6:2; Mark 12:38-40; John 11:47, 48; 19:15) Jesus plainly told such "money lovers" that they were disgusting in God's sight, because they were hypocrites. He likened them to "whitewashed graves, which outwardly indeed appear beautiful but inside are full of dead men's bones and of every sort of uncleanness," and then

---

28. How does this practice stand in contrast to the teachings of Jesus Christ and his apostles?
29. What similarities do you see between the world's religious leaders in our day and the ones who opposed Jesus in the first century C.E.?

said to them: "In that way you also, outwardly indeed, appear righteous to men, but inside you are full of hypocrisy and lawlessness."—Luke 16:14, 15; Matthew 23:27, 28.

IN WHAT HAS REJECTION OF THE BIBLE RESULTED?

[30] To the people of Israel, a nation that claimed to worship him, Jehovah God is recorded as saying: "I, Jehovah, am your God, the One teaching you to benefit yourself . . . O if only you would actually pay attention to my commandments! Then your peace would become just like a river, and your righteousness like the waves of the sea."—Isaiah 48:17, 18.

[31] But the evidence considered shows that the world's religions have not paid attention to God's commandments. In Christendom, in fact, more and more clergymen are openly expressing their lack of faith in the Bible as the inspired Word of God. *Science* magazine of November 1972 describes a California board of education meeting in which a "Mormon bishop and the dean of San Francisco's Grace Episcopal Cathedral" argued in favor of evolution as against the creation account in the Bible book of Genesis.[20]

[32] The *New Catholic Encyclopedia,* while claiming to accept essentially the Bible as inspired, says: "It is nonetheless obvious that many Biblical statements are simply not true when judged according to modern knowledge of science and history."[21]

[33] A similar viewpoint is expressed in the Baptist

30. As shown in Isaiah 48:17, 18, what is the result when people pay attention to Jehovah's commandments?
31-33. What is here shown as to the attitude of many clergymen toward the Word of God?

Broadman Bible Commentary.[22] At a 1972 convention of the Southern Baptists (the largest Protestant denomination in the United States), a resolution was presented to recall and rewrite this work because it did not uphold the Bible's truthfulness. But the resolution was voted down by a ratio of about 4 to 1.—*The Christian Century,* August 2, 1972.

[34] What have been the results of all this? Have the world's religions been able to demonstrate that they can downgrade Bible teachings and still produce good morals, conducive to peace and security? To the contrary, conditions worsen earth wide, and Christendom has long been among the hardest hit as to crime, immorality, drug addiction, racial strife and war. The nations with non-Christian religions have also become increasingly the scene of unrest and division, political corruption and deteriorating morals. As the Bible puts it: "They have rejected the very word of Jehovah, and what wisdom do they have?" —Jeremiah 8:9.

[35] The evidence world wide is undeniable. It proves that the world's religions are not a true force for peace and security. What does this signify for us?

END OF WORLD'S RELIGIONS NEARS

[36] Jesus Christ stated: "Every plant that my heavenly Father did not plant will be uprooted." (Matthew 15:13) Their bad fruitage proves that the world's religions are not of God's planting.

34, 35. (a) What have been the results of rejecting the teachings of the Bible? (b) So, can we reasonably look to the world's religions to lead mankind to peace and security?
36, 37. What does the Bible warn will come upon the world's religions?

Even as the Bible warned that such religions would never bring peaceful, righteous conditions, so too it warns of the coming destruction of all false systems of worship.

[37] Speaking of it under the symbol of the harlotrous "Babylon the Great," God says of such religious empire:

"Her sins have massed together clear up to heaven, and God has called her acts of injustice to mind. . . . in one day her plagues will come, death and mourning and famine, and she will be completely burned with fire, because Jehovah God, who judged her, is strong."—Revelation 18:5-8.

[38] Note that the destruction of the world empire of false religion is to come with surprising suddenness, as "in one day." All the riches she has piled up will be devastated by the political nations, to the surprise and dismay of many persons. —Revelation 18:10-17, 21; 17:12, 16.

[39] Therefore the divine call is: "Get out of her, my people, if you do not want to share with her in her sins, and if you do not want to receive part of her plagues." (Revelation 18:4) To take such action means for you to see this world empire of false religion as God sees it, and detest it for its rotten fruits, its hypocrisy and superstition. Disgust should be felt for the way "Babylon the Great" has misrepresented God before mankind and for the suffering, oppression and grinding down of the people to which this has contributed. (Romans 2:24; Jeremiah 23:21, 22) If you recognize this, you will withdraw all support from her, thus demonstrating your full support of God's judgment on her.

---

38. How will such destruction come, and from what source?
39. (a) At Revelation 18:4, what are persons who desire God's approval urged to do? (b) What moves them to take such action?

⁴⁰ It is not enough simply to withdraw, however, if you seek a peaceful, secure life for yourself and your family. You must search out and find now the true, unhypocritical worship that will bring you God's peace and protection when the foretold destruction comes. Those engaging in such true worship must be persons who have already 'beaten their swords into plowshares, not learning war anymore.' (Isaiah 2:4) They must be persons who believe God's Word and genuinely live it, letting it be the guiding force in their lives. (Psalm 119:105 [118:105, *Dy*]) They must show genuine, unhypocritical love for their fellowman. (John 13:35; Romans 13:8) There are such people today. And the peace and security they enjoy vindicate the truthfulness and power of God's Word, the Bible.

⁴¹ Those through whom you received this book, Jehovah's Christian witnesses, are keenly concerned about the dangerous situation into which false religion has brought the people. They themselves are sincerely endeavoring to give God's Word first place in their lives. You are invited to attend their meetings in their local Kingdom Hall and investigate for yourself the extent to which they show the fruitage of God's spirit and enjoy the peace and security it brings. You will also see how they are learning and applying what God requires of every person who is to survive into His righteous new order.

40. (a) Additionally, what must a person find, if he is to enjoy a peaceful, secure life? (b) What kind of persons should one look for when seeking to find those who practice true worship?
41. What will you be able to observe firsthand by attending the meetings of Jehovah's witnesses at their Kingdom Hall?

CHAPTER 4

World Destruction First
—Then World Peace

A CCORDING to Bible prophecy, before mankind can ever enjoy enduring peace, a world destruction must first take place. Why should that be? From what source is the destruction foretold to come? And with what results for humans on this planet?

² We should first recognize that the world destruction the Bible foretells is not the same as the global catastrophe that certain world leaders, scientists and others are warning about. The calamity they talk about would come in the form of widespread famine, pestilence, pollution or nuclear war or some combination of these. But such a catastrophe would never pave the way for lasting peace and security on this planet. Why not?

³ Because it would either ruin the planet entirely for all living creatures, as by radiation pollution through an all-out war, or it would leave as survivors persons who would be no better—if not possibly worse—than those who would die. Survival would be largely a matter of chance, though the poor would seem likely to be among the first to suffer. What sure hope would *you* have of being among the survivors of such a world catastrophe?

1-3. (a) What is the world destruction that human leaders are warning about? (b) Why is that not what the Bible refers to as the world destruction that will pave the way for lasting peace and security on this earth?

Even if you were among those surviving, what hope could you have that life would not drift back into the same strife-ridden uncertainty that now prevails?

WHAT THE BIBLE FORETELLS GIVES HOPE

⁴ The world destruction the Bible foretells is to be selective, purposeful. It is not some calamity that comes just as "the culmination of man's timeless errors." Rather than bring death to just anyone indiscriminately, it will cleanse the earth of those who really deserve destruction, who bear responsibility for the bad conditions on earth. It will harmonize with the divine principle at Proverbs 2:21, 22:

> "For the upright are the ones that will reside in the earth, and the blameless are the ones that will be left over in it. As regards the wicked, they will be cut off from the very earth; and as for the treacherous, they will be torn away from it."

⁵ What, then, will be destroyed? Many think the Bible predicts the total burning up of the planet Earth and everything on it. But this is not the case. Jesus Christ himself said: "Happy are the mild-tempered ones, since they will inherit the earth." (Matthew 5:5) Surely that 'inheritance' is not to be a burned-up, lifeless cinder! The Bible also gives God's definite assurance that the earth will remain forever as a place for people to live.—Psalm 104:5 [103:5, *Dy*]; Isaiah 45:18; Matthew 6:9, 10.

⁶ In harmony with this, the Bible speaks of the

---

4. Who are to be destroyed in the world destruction of which the Bible speaks?
5, 6. (a) What will happen to the earth itself during that world destruction? (b) In this respect, how will it be "just as the days of Noah were"?

survivors who will remain on earth after that destruction has passed. (Revelation 7:9, 10, 13, 14) Jesus Christ said that "just as the days of Noah were, so the presence of the Son of man will be." When global destruction took place in Noah's time there were also survivors.—Matthew 24:37; 2 Peter 2:5, 9.

7 What is to be destroyed, then, is the *worldwide system of things* that men have built up on earth —along with all those who uphold it rather than looking to God and his promised rule for the earth. (Psalm 73:27, 28 [72:27, 28, *Dy*]) That is why, instead of the phrase "the end of the world," found in some translations of the Bible, other translations more accurately render the original-language (Greek) expression as "the end of the age" (*NE*), "the conclusion of the age" (*Ro*), "the conclusion of the system of things" (*NW*). —Matthew 24:3.

8 The *source* of the coming world destruction will be—not men—but Jehovah God. The modern crises of pollution, famine and similar things that have resulted from human ignorance, error and corruption are not what will cause the destruction. Instead, these are proof of the selfishness and utter failure of the present world system. They provide just cause for Jehovah God to do away with that system completely. He promises to take such action before ever the present world system reaches a state of collapse or carries out its own self-destruction. (Revelation 11:17, 18) But is such drastic action really the only way?

---

7. What is it that will come to its end at that time?
8. (a) From what source will the destruction come? (b) This must occur before the present world system reaches what state?

WHY THIS WORLD SYSTEM MUST END
FOR TRUE PEACE TO COME

[9] It might seem to some that God could simply make some changes in the present world system, rather than totally destroying it. But the Bible shows that God realistically recognizes that this world system of things is beyond reform.

[10] Consider for yourself the hundreds of changes that have been made by humans down through the centuries. Think of all the different kinds of government that men have developed—city-states, monarchies, democracies, communistic and socialistic governments, even dictatorships. Remember how often the existing ruler, or the entire government, has been deposed and replaced with a new one—by election, by coup d'etat, by revolution —but with no lasting solution to the problems of mankind. Even well-meaning men who try to improve man's lot find their efforts blocked by the world system into which they themselves are locked. As a wise ruler of ancient times discovered, by human efforts alone "that which is made crooked cannot be made straight."—Ecclesiastes 1:14, 15.

[11] The world's cities, for example, are plagued with problems, but men cannot dismantle them and start afresh. The same is true of the whole economic and industrial systems of the world. Self-interest and nationalism undermine and block any real change for the good of mankind as a whole.

[12] The entire world system is thus like a house

9, 10. How does human history show that something more drastic is needed than just a reform of the present world system?

11-13. (a) What prevents men from making changes in the present system for the good of all mankind? (b) So, how might the extent of the change needed be illustrated?

built on a bad foundation from poor plans and
with defective materials. What good will it do to
rearrange the furniture or to repair or remodel
the house? As long as it stands, the problems will
continue and the house will keep deteriorating.
The only sensible thing to do is to tear it down and
build another, on a good foundation.

[13] Jesus Christ used a somewhat similar illustration in saying that people do not "put new wine
into old wineskins." The old wineskin would burst
from the new wine. (Matthew 9:17) He therefore
did not try to reform the Jewish system of things
under which he lived, but preached God's kingdom
as the only hope for peace and security. (Luke
8:1; 11:2; 12:31) So, too, in our day Jehovah God
will not simply dress up or adjust the present
world's system, because that could bring no lasting
benefit.

[14] God's Word emphasizes the truth that it is
impossible to legislate righteousness into people's
hearts. If they have no love for what is right, no
amount of legislation will ever put it there. At
Isaiah 26:10 we read: "Though the wicked one
should be shown favor, he simply will not learn
righteousness. In the land of straightforwardness
he will act unjustly and will not see the eminence
of Jehovah."—Compare Proverbs 29:1.

[15] The hard fact is that many people prefer to
stay with this present system despite its failures
and evils—rather than turn to righteousness and
submit to rule from God. Though seeing the
corruption and deception of its political systems,
the futility of its wars, the hypocrisy of the

---

14. Would the passing of new laws make people love righteousness?
15, 16. How is the lack of true love for righteousness on the part
of many people shown in their response to God's will?

world's religions and the clear evidence that its scientific technology has created even greater problems than it has solved—despite all this, many refuse to look to God and his kingdom as the true source of peace and security. They are like the Israelites of whom God said: "The prophets themselves actually prophesy in falsehood; and as for the priests, they go subduing according to their powers. And my own people *have loved it that way;* and what will you men do in the finale of it?" —Jeremiah 5:31; Isaiah 30:12, 13.

[16] Although you may find this difficult to understand, you yourself have seen how persons will ignore all evidence that a certain course is ruinous. You have doubtless seen persons who keep up certain practices or habits that they know are endangering their own health and security and that of their families, and they resist all human efforts to help them change. But when persons resist God's counsel and guidance, this becomes far more serious. Persons who do this show that they really do not love truth and righteousness. Hence the Bible says about such ones: "For God's wrath is being revealed from heaven against all ungodliness and unrighteousness of men who are suppressing the truth in an unrighteous way . . . For his invisible qualities are clearly seen from the world's creation onward, because they are perceived by the things made, even his eternal power and Godship, so that they are inexcusable." (Romans 1:18-20) Of similar ones, Jesus Christ said: "For the heart of this people has grown unreceptive, and with their ears they have heard without response, and they have shut their eyes; that they might never see with their eyes and hear with their ears and get the sense of it with

their hearts and turn back, and [God] heal them."
—Matthew 13:15.

[17] Rightly, God's patience and mercy have their
limits. If not, where would his love for the righteous ones be? He cannot turn a deaf ear to their
pleas for relief from the suffering that wickedness
brings upon this earth. (Luke 18:7, 8; Proverbs
29:2, 16) So, the circumstances require world
destruction; they oblige God to do so if he is to
remain true to what is right and just and is to
show compassion for those who also love what is
right. Yet it is not a case of God's taking pleasure
in bringing destruction upon mankind. As he
says: " 'Do I take any delight at all in the death
of someone wicked,' is the utterance of the Sovereign Lord Jehovah, 'and not in that he should
turn back from his ways and actually keep living?'
. . . 'So cause a turning back and keep living, O
you people.' "—Ezekiel 18:23, 32.

[18] The destruction of those staying with this
present world system, then, is the price that must
be paid to redeem from insecurity and suffering
those who love what is right. This is in harmony
with the Bible principle: "The wicked is a ransom
for the righteous one."—Proverbs 21:18; compare
Isaiah 43:1, 3, 4.

BENEFICIAL RESULTS

[19] What will result from the destruction of the
present world system and its supporters? This
will allow for a righteous rule earth wide in which

---

17. If it is true that God does not take pleasure in bringing destruction on mankind, why is he going to do it?
18. What is the price that must be paid to redeem from insecurity
the people who love what is right?
19. What barriers to world peace will be removed by the destruction of this system of things?

the survivors will be able to work together united-
ly, not in selfish competition. Down will come
divisive national frontiers and political boundaries.
Down will come tariff walls and tax barriers.
Gone will be the crushing burden of military
spending. And gone too will be the social barriers
that keep mankind from being a united family
on earth. A vital factor in all this will be that all
then living will speak the 'one pure language' of
truth to one another, worshiping their Creator
"with spirit and truth," undivided by religious
superstitions, traditions and man-made creeds.
—Zephaniah 3:8, 9 [Sophonias 3:8, 9, *Dy*]; John
4:23, 24.

[20] With God's government by his Son Christ
Jesus exercising sole dominion over all the earth,
the ancient psalm of the Bible will see a fulfillment
far greater than in the days of ancient Israel:
"In his days the righteous one will sprout, and the
abundance of peace until the moon is no more.
And he will have subjects from sea to sea and
from the River to the ends of the earth."—Psalm
72:7, 8 [71:7, 8, *Dy*].

[21] Earth itself will benefit from the coming
world destruction. It will no longer be marred
and stained by greedy polluters and ruthless de-
stroyers. The lakes, rivers and oceans as well as
the atmosphere will gain relief from all the wastes
poured into them and will soon cleanse themselves.
God will thus demonstrate that he has not abandoned his original purpose to have a clean, garden-
like planet filled with people who reflect their

20. As indicated by Psalm 72, what condition will come to be
earth wide?
21. How will the earth itself benefit from the coming world
destruction?

Creator's own splendid qualities.—Genesis 1:26-28; Isaiah 45:18; 55:10, 11.

[22] So, God's bringing world destruction is not contrary to his being the 'God of peace,' nor contrary to his Messianic king Jesus' being the "Prince of Peace." It is because of their love of peace and justice that they take this action to restore earth to a clean, righteous state.—1 Corinthians 14:33; Isaiah 9:6, 7.

[23] As individuals, then, what can we do? Jesus Christ showed that those ignoring God's instructions, which Jesus taught, were building their personal hopes for the future on "sand" and that such building would never endure destructive storms of adversity. He showed the vital need to build our hopes on obedience to God's Word if we are to have a peaceful and secure future. —Matthew 7:24-27.

[24] But why has God waited till now to take action to bring wickedness and suffering to an end? The Bible answers this question also and shows what God has been doing during all the centuries past in working out his purpose.

---

22. How is the bringing of such destruction consistent with God's being a 'God of peace'?
23, 24. If we are to enjoy a future of peace and security, what is it vital for us individually to do now?

CHAPTER 5

An Issue That Involves You

DESPITE the common desire for peace and security, man's history almost from its start has been marred by bloodshed and other badness. Since the Bible shows that God detests such things, why has he not put a stop to these conditions before now? Surely it cannot be for lack of interest. The Bible, as well as the beauty of God's earthly handiwork, gives abundant evidence of his love and concern for mankind. (1 John 4:8) More importantly, the honor of God's own name is involved, since these conditions have caused people to reproach him. What reason could there be, then, for his putting up with thousands of years of unrest and violence?

[2] The answer is found in the opening book of the Bible, in what it says about Adam and Eve. This account is no mere allegory. It is historical fact. The Bible supplies a complete, documented record of genealogy reaching from the first century of the Common Era all the way back to the first man. (Luke 3:23-38; Genesis 5:1-32; 11:10-32) As our forefather, Adam had an influence on us. And what the Bible tells us about him helps us to understand the circumstances that affect our lives today.

[3] The Bible reveals that all of God's provisions

1. Why have people found it difficult to understand why God has permitted badness among mankind?
2. (a) Where in the Bible do we find out why God has permitted bad conditions for so long? (b) What makes it evident that the Bible account about Adam and Eve is historical fact?
3. What kind of provisions did God make for mankind at the start?

for the first human couple were very good. They
had everything for a happy life—a parklike home
in the region called Eden, abundant varieties of
food, satisfying work, the prospect of seeing their
family grow and fill the earth, and the blessing
of their Creator. (Genesis 1:28, 29; 2:8, 9, 15)
Who could reasonably have asked for more?

⁴ The inspired record in Genesis reveals that
man occupied a unique position on earth. Man
alone was made "in God's image." (Genesis 1:27)
Unlike the animals, he had a heart possessed of
moral sense and he was endowed with free will.
That is why he was equipped with powers of
reason and judgment. To guide man, God im-
planted in Adam the faculty of conscience so that,
as a perfect man in his Creator's "image," his
normal inclination would be toward good. (Romans 2:15) Besides all this, God spoke to his
earthly son, telling him why he was alive, what
he was to do and who had provided all the splendid
things around him. (Genesis 1:28-30) How, then,
do we explain the bad conditions that now exist?

⁵ The Scriptural record shows that an issue
arose—one that involves each of us today. It
came about through circumstances that developed
not long after the creation of the first human
pair. God gave man the opportunity to demonstrate loving appreciation to his Creator by obedience to a simple requirement. The requirement
was nothing that would imply that man had in-
considerate or even depraved tendencies that had

<hr/>

4. (a) At his creation, in what ways was man different from other
earthly creatures? (b) In what manner was needed guidance
provided for Adam?
5. (a) What simple requirement did God lay upon the man, and
for what reason? (b) Why were man's life prospects for the
future rightly involved?

to be curbed. Rather, it involved something that in itself was normal and proper—the eating of food. As God told the man: "From every tree of the garden you may eat to satisfaction. But as for the tree of the knowledge of good and bad you must not eat from it, for in the day you eat from it you will positively die." (Genesis 2:16, 17) This requirement did not deprive man of anything necessary for life; he could eat from all the other trees in the garden. Yet his life prospects for the *future* were definitely involved, and rightly so. Why? Because the One who stated that commandment was the very Source and Sustainer of man's life.

⁶ God's purpose was not for man to die. No mention of death was made to Adam except as punishment for disobedience. Our first parents had before them the grand prospect of living forever in their peaceful, parklike home. To attain to this, what was required of them? Simply that they recognize that the earth on which they lived belongs to God, the One who made it, and that, as the Creator, God is the rightful Ruler of his creation. (Psalm 24:1, 10 [23:1, 10, *Dy*]) Surely this One, who had given man everything he had, even life itself, deserved appreciative obedience to any requirement that he might lay upon the man. That obedience was not to be forced, however. It must be motivated by love. —1 John 5:3.

⁷ Adam failed to show such love. How did this come about?

6, 7. (a) Our first parents could have lived forever if they had acted in harmony with what basic truth regarding rulership? (b) Why should Adam have felt moved to obey God?

THE ORIGIN OF RESISTANCE TO DIVINE RULE

[8] The Bible shows that resistance to God's rulership first began, not on earth, but in the spirit realm, a realm invisible to human eyes. Should we, like many, doubt the existence of that realm simply because it is invisible to us? No; that would not be reasonable. Gravity cannot be seen, neither can the wind. Yet their effects can be. So, too, the effects of the spirit realm can be observed. "God is a Spirit," and his works of creation are all around us. If we believe in him, we are obliged to believe in a spirit realm. (John 4:24; Romans 1:20) But who else inhabits that realm?

[9] Millions of spirit persons, angels, were brought into existence before man. (Psalm 103:20 [102:20, Dy]) All these were created perfect; none with evil tendencies. Yet, like God's later creation man, they were granted free will. They could therefore choose a course of faithfulness or of unfaithfulness toward God.

[10] But the question asked by many persons is: How, as perfect creatures, could any of them even feel inclined to do wrong? Well, we ourselves know how in our own lives a circumstance can arise that confronts us with various possibilities —some good, some bad. That we have the intelligence to discern the bad possibilities does not automatically make us bad, does it? The real question is: On which course will we fix our mind and heart? If we were to hold on to thoughts of

8. (a) Where does the Bible show that resistance to God's rulership began? (b) Why is it reasonable to believe in the spirit realm?
9. What kind of persons are the angels?
10, 11. (a) How is it possible for a perfect spirit creature to feel inclined to do wrong? (b) So, how did one of the angels come to be Satan?

what is bad, that would draw us into cultivating wrong desire in our hearts, and this desire would move us eventually to commit wrong acts. That is how the Bible writer James explains the way sin is born. "Each one is tried by being drawn out and enticed by his own desire. Then the desire, when it has become fertile, gives birth to sin; in turn, sin, when it has been accomplished, brings forth death."—James 1:14, 15.

¹¹ The Scriptures reveal that one of God's spirit sons allowed wrong desire to develop in him. He saw the possibility that God's human creation could come into submission to him rather than to God, and evidently he began to crave at least a share in the worship that was rendered to God. (Luke 4:5-8) Acting in harmony with his desire, he became a resister of God. For that reason he is referred to in the Bible as Satan, which means Resister.—Job 1:6.

¹² It is true that, in this materialistic twentieth century, belief in such a spirit person as Satan is not popular. But, then, popularity has never been a sure guide to truth. Among those who study disease, it was once unpopular to believe that unseen germs were a factor to consider, but now their influence is well known. Certainly, if what is popular had always been a true guide by which to live, this world would be in far different condition than it is now. Jesus Christ, who himself had come from the spirit realm, could speak with authority on life there. He definitely referred to Satan as a spirit person whose influence could bring severe trials in people's lives. (John 8:23; Luke 13:16; 22:31) Only by taking into account

12. What sound basis is there for believing that Satan really does exist?

the existence of this spirit Adversary can we understand how bad conditions got started on this earth.

[13] The inspired record, in Genesis chapter 3, describes how he proceeded in an endeavor to satisfy his wrong desire. In the Garden of Eden, he approached the woman Eve, but doing so in a deceptive manner so as to conceal his real identity. He was invisible to her eyes, and as yet he had no human agent through whom he could work; so the record shows that he employed an animal commonly seen by the human pair—a serpent. Evidently using what we would call ventriloquism, he made it appear that his words proceeded from this creature, whose naturally cautious manner fit well with the impression that he wanted to make. —Genesis 3:1; Revelation 12:9.

[14] Rather than make a direct bid for the woman to look to him as her ruler, Satan first sought to plant doubt in her mind, asking: "Is it really so that God said you must not eat from every tree of the garden?" In effect, he was saying: 'It is a pity that God has said you may not eat from all the trees in the garden.' By this he inferred that possibly God was holding back something good. Eve answered by quoting God's prohibition, which involved only one tree, as well as stating the death penalty that disobedience would bring. At that, Satan attempted to undermine respect for God's law, saying: "You positively will not die. For God knows that in the very day of your eating from it your eyes are bound to be opened and you are bound to be like God, knowing good and bad."

---

13. How did Satan communicate with the woman Eve, and why in that manner?
14. What did Satan say to Eve, and with what evident intent?

(Genesis 3:1-5) Faced with such a situation, what would you have done?

¹⁵ The Bible record shows that Eve allowed herself to be drawn along by selfish desire, and she ate what God had forbidden. Afterward, under her urging, her husband Adam also ate, choosing to cast his lot in with her rather than with his Creator. What was the outcome?—Genesis 3:6; 1 Timothy 2:14.

¹⁶ The entire human family was plunged into sin and imperfection. Adam now could not pass on to his offspring the perfection that he no longer had. As in making copies of something from a mold or pattern that is itself defective—all the copies will have the same defect. So, all Adam's offspring were born in sin, with an inherited tendency toward selfishness. (Genesis 8:21) It is this inclination, left unchecked, that has led to theft, rape, murder and all the other badness that has taken peace and security from mankind. It is this inheritance of sin that has also resulted in disease and death.—Romans 5:12.

THE ISSUE RAISED

¹⁷ In the light of these facts, our minds go back to the question raised earlier: Why has God put up with this situation, allowing it to develop to the extent that it has? It is because of the issue that was raised and its effect on the entire universe. How is that so?

¹⁸ By his argument that God's law to Adam was

---

15. (a) Why did Eve fall victim to Satan? (b) What did Adam do?

16. So, then, what accounts for the crime and violence, as well as the disease and death, that have marked human existence since the time of Adam?

17, 18. (a) To understand why God has put up with this situation for so long, what important issue must we appreciate? (b) What really is the issue that was raised?

not good for man and by challenging what God said would be the outcome for disobedience, Satan was calling into question God's rulership. He did not question the fact that God is ruler. Rather, the issue that Satan raised centered on the *rightfulness* of Jehovah's rulership and the *righteousness* of His ways. Deceptively, Satan argued that man would make out better by acting independently, making his own decisions rather than submitting to God's direction. (Genesis 3:4, 5) In reality, however, by so doing man would be following the leading of God's adversary.

[19] Another matter was involved. Since these creatures of God turned against him there in Eden, what would the others do? Later, in the days of the man Job, Satan openly charged that those who serve Jehovah do so, not because of any love for God and his rulership, but selfishly, because God provides everything for them. Satan inferred that, when put under pressure, no one would prove to be a loyal supporter of Jehovah's sovereignty. The loyalty and integrity of every intelligent creature in heaven and on earth were called into question. The issue thus involves you. —Job 1:8-12; 2:4, 5.

[20] Faced with such a challenge, what would Jehovah do? He could easily, and rightfully, have destroyed Satan and Adam and Eve at the time of the rebellion in Eden. That would have demonstrated Jehovah's sovereign power. But would it have answered the questions now raised in the minds of all God's creatures who had observed these developments? The eternal peace and secu-

19. (a) What else was involved in the issue, and where is this shown in the Bible? (b) How does this issue involve us?
20, 21. By deferring destruction of the rebels, what opportunity did Jehovah afford his creatures, both angels and humans?

rity of the universe required that these questions be settled completely, once and for all time. Besides that, the integrity and loyalty of all God's intelligent creation had been called into question. If they truly loved him, they would want to answer that false charge themselves. Jehovah determined to afford them opportunity to do just that and to show their real heart attitude toward his sovereign rule. Also, by allowing Adam and Eve to bring forth offspring (though imperfect), God would prevent the extinction of the human family as yet unborn—a family that has come to include all of us living today. This would give these descendants the opportunity to choose for themselves whether they would obey divine rulership. That choice is what now confronts you!

²¹ So, instead of executing the death penalty at once in Eden, Jehovah allowed those rebelling to remain for a time. Adam and Eve were expelled from Eden, to die before a thousand years passed. (Genesis 5:5; compare Genesis 2:17 with 2 Peter 3:8.) Satan was also to be destroyed in due time, as if he were a serpent whose head had been crushed.—Genesis 3:15; Romans 16:20.

WHAT THE PASSING OF TIME HAS REVEALED

²² What has resulted from God's accepting the challenge as to the rightfulness of his sovereignty? Has man benefited himself by listening to God's adversary and endeavoring to run his own affairs? Satan has been permitted to build up "wicked spirit forces," organizing them into 'governments and authorities and world rulers.' (Ephesians

---

22, 23. (a) As to rulership, what have Satan and mankind been doing during the time allowed by God? (b) What does human history for the past six thousand years show as to government that endeavors to ignore God?

6:11, 12) Mankind has been granted opportunity to try every conceivable type of government. Jehovah did not allow only a few generations to come and go and then put a stop to man's efforts before the full results could be seen. Even a century ago would have been too soon. Man was then just entering the "era of technology" and was only beginning to make great claims about what he would now accomplish.

²³ But now, is another century needed to see what the outcome of man's course of independence from God will be? Even prominent men in fields of government and science acknowledge that, judged by present trends, the earth and life upon it now face grave danger of ruination. Certainly God does not need to permit complete ruin in order to prove the utter failure of man's independent rule. With the testimony of six thousand years bearing witness to the results of government that endeavors to ignore God, never can men— or spirit rebels either—say they did not have enough time to prove their challenge. The facts show that no government independent of God can bring real peace and security for all mankind.

²⁴ As we will later see, long in advance and with perfect timing Jehovah God marked this generation as the one during which he would cleanse the universe of all rebellion against his divine rulership. Not only would wicked men be forever destroyed, but Satan and his demons would be restrained as in an abyss, unable to influence the affairs of either men or angels. This is to open the way for the righteous rule of earth by the government of God's Son. During a period of a

24. What is soon to take place, to clear the way for righteous rule of the earth by God's Son?

thousand years, that government will undo all the harm brought by man's thousands of years of selfish rule. It will restore this earth to paradisaic loveliness and bring obedient mankind back to the perfection enjoyed in Eden.—Revelation 20:1, 2; 21:1-5; 1 Corinthians 15:25, 26.

[25] At the close of that thousand-year rule, the Bible states that God's adversary and his demons will be released from their restraint for a brief time. Why? In order that all those then living may have the opportunity and privilege of giving a final, resounding answer to the challenging issue raised, showing themselves to be wholeheartedly in favor of and loyal to Jehovah God's sovereign rule. Untold numbers will have come forth in the resurrection. For many of them this will be their first opportunity to demonstrate under test their devotion and love for the Life-Giver, Jehovah God. And even those who in the past stood up under tests in an imperfect state, and amid the bad conditions of this present system, will then be able to do so in human perfection and in surroundings similar to those of Eden. The issue will be the same as raised there in Eden— whether they as individuals will uphold Jehovah's sovereignty by faithful obedience and unbreakable integrity to his expressed will. Jehovah God desires as his subjects only those who have the love that motivates such devotion. Those who wish to side with God's adversary and his demons in whatever vain attempts these make to disturb anew the peace of God's universe will be free to make that choice. But by thus spurning govern-

---

25. (a) Why are Satan and his demons to be released at the end of a thousand years? (b) What will the outcome be?

ment by God they will merit destruction, and this time it will come promptly, as if by fire from heaven. All rebels, spirit and human, will then have perished for all time.—Revelation 20:7-10.

[26] True, for thousands of years mankind has suffered much hardship. But this was due to the first man's choice, not God's. God has endured reproach and has put up with things detestable to him for all this time. But God, for whom 'a thousand years is as one day,' is able to take a long-range view of matters and this works out for the good of his creatures. As the inspired apostle writes: "Jehovah is not slow respecting his promise, as some people consider slowness, but he is patient with you because he does not desire any to be destroyed but desires all to attain to repentance." (2 Peter 3:9) Had it not been for God's patience and long-suffering, what opportunity for salvation would any of us today have had?

[27] However, we should not conclude that during the past six thousand years God's role has been merely a passive one, that he has simply been tolerating the wickedness that has developed but taking no action himself. As we shall see, the facts show just the opposite.

26, 27. How has Jehovah's handling of matters really worked out for the benefit of each one of us?

CHAPTER 6

What Has God Been Doing?

IN RECENT years some people, notably religious leaders, have been saying that "God is dead." Do they mean that God does not exist? Not in most cases. Usually they mean that they do not believe that he is actively interested in the earth or is doing anything about the problems troubling mankind. But the truth is that God is very much alive, that he does care. True, he may not have done what men expected him to do. But this does not mean he has done nothing. Actually, he has been active on behalf of mankind from the beginning of human history right down to the present day.

² One reason for the feeling of some persons that "God is dead" is man's short life-span. This makes man impatient to get things done in the brief time that life allows him. Sometimes his efforts prove premature, and so fail to achieve the intended goal. But his desire to see results during his own lifetime dominates his thinking. Mistakenly, he tends to judge God on the basis of such human experience, with all its limitations.

³ On the other hand, Jehovah lives forever. (Psalm 102:24 [101:25, Dy]; Isaiah 44:6) He does not need to become impatient. He can scan the situation and see precisely where in the

---

1. (a) When people say that "God is dead," what do they mean? (b) Do you agree with them?
2. How may the shortness of a man's life affect his thinking on this matter?
3. How does the length of Jehovah's life affect his ability to handle situations at the best possible time?

stream of time his acts will accomplish the most good for everyone concerned, as well as for the effective development of his purpose. (Isaiah 40:22; 2 Peter 3:8, 9) That is exactly what God has done.

HOW GOD HAS REVEALED HIMSELF

[4] Jehovah's declared purpose is to provide a righteous administration for all creation, one that will enable mankind to live in peace and unity, with the enjoyment of full security. (Ephesians 1:9, 10; Proverbs 1:33) However, God does not force anyone to serve him. He gathers under his administration only those who willingly acknowledge his position and who love his rulership. With a view to laying a foundation for an entire world of mankind that would live in harmony with his requirements, God proceeded to provide mankind with knowledge of the standards and principles of his righteous administration and how it operates. At the same time he was making it possible for mankind to gain vital knowledge concerning God himself and his personal qualities. —John 17:3.

[5] Being spirit, Jehovah is, of course, invisible to man. So, how would he make men of flesh and blood understand these things? Much can be learned about the qualities of the Creator from his handiwork. (Romans 1:20) The marvelous interrelationship of the earthly processes of life bears testimony to his wisdom. The tremendous power manifest in the oceans, in the weather and in the controlled movement of the heavenly bodies gives evidence of his almightiness. (Job 38:8-11,

4. What has Jehovah declared his purpose to be, and so what knowledge has he provided for mankind?
5. From the works of creation, what can we learn about God?

22-33; 40:2) And the variety of foods that the earth yields, along with the beauty of flowers, birds, sunrises and sunsets, and the playful antics of animals, all tell of the Creator's love for mankind and his desire that we find enjoyment in life. Yet God's revelation of himself does not stop with these things.

⁶ On various occasions he has also spoken from the heavens, in some cases personally, and in other instances through angels. Thus, he has gradually acquainted man with His righteous standards and His will. He did this at Mount Sinai on the Arabian Peninsula, where he spoke in an awe-inspiring manner, giving his law to the millions of Israelites who had gathered there. (Exodus 19:16-19; 20:22) Then, by means of his prophets he communicated with men over a period of many centuries, and he had them write down the revelations of his will. (2 Peter 1:21) Besides this, God has chosen to reveal his principles and qualities by having dealings with his people, thereby adding the warm appeal of human experience to his inspired recorded Word. How much more instructive, convincing and moving not only to hear and read God's declarations of purpose, but also to be able to see in the inerasable historical record examples that enable us to understand his will for us. (1 Corinthians 10:11) What does that record reveal?

⁷ It provides man with the evidence that *God does not forever tolerate unrighteousness.* True,

------

6. (a) By what means has God provided specific revelations of his will? (b) By what other means has God revealed his principles and qualities to man?
7. (a) How has God demonstrated that he does not forever tolerate unrighteousness? (b) On learning how God views such conduct, what should we do?

he let the offspring of Adam go their own way, building up the inevitable record of man's inability to govern himself successfully. But God did not leave mankind without evidence of His judgment against their unrighteous ways. Thus he brought a flood in Noah's day because 'the earth had become full of violence.' (Genesis 6:11-13) He destroyed the sexually depraved cities of Sodom and Gomorrah. (Genesis 19:24; Jude 7) He let the nation of Israel, which professed to serve him, go into exile because they practiced falsehood. (Jeremiah 13:19, 25) On learning how God views such conduct, we have the opportunity to make changes in our lives to show our love of righteousness. Will we?

[8] A further vital point that the record reveals to man is that God does not sweep away the righteous with the wicked. In the global flood, God did not destroy Noah, who was a "preacher of righteousness," but spared him and seven others. (2 Peter 2:5) And, before fire and sulphur rained down on Sodom, escape was made possible for righteous Lot and his household.—Genesis 19:15-17; 2 Peter 2:7.

[9] When the people of Israel, who were in a covenant relationship with God, proved unfaithful to him, what did he do? He did not at once cast them off. As he told them by means of his prophet Jeremiah: "I kept sending to you all my servants the prophets, daily getting up early and sending them." But they did not listen. (Jeremiah 7:25, 26) Even as the time for the actual siege

---

8. When God brings destruction, are there any survivors? Illustrate.
9, 10. (a) How do you react to the way that Jehovah dealt with Israel, in view of his urging them again and again to turn away from badness? (b) Besides his being patient, what else do these accounts teach us about God?

and destruction of Jerusalem drew near, Jehovah
spoke through his prophet Ezekiel, saying: " 'Do
I take any delight at all in the death of someone
wicked,' is the utterance of the Sovereign Lord
Jehovah, 'and not in that he should turn back
from his ways and actually keep living? . . . So
cause a turning back and keep living, O you
people.' "—Ezekiel 18:23, 32.

¹⁰ What do we see, then? That, in a manner
that deeply touches the heart of righteously dis-
posed persons, Jehovah has made clear his great
patience with mankind. At the same time, by his
dealings he also forcefully impresses on us his love
of righteousness and the importance of living in
harmony with his requirements.

¹¹ Something else, very basic, is made to stand
out. From the beginning, we see that God has had
a definite *purpose* in everything that he has done,
and he has never failed to act when the accomplishment of his purpose required action. His
fundamental purpose was stated, though in veiled
language, right in Eden. When passing judgment
on Satan, Jehovah foretold that Satan would
have opportunity to raise up a "seed," those who
would manifest his traits and do his will. He also
foretold the producing of another "seed," a righteous deliverer. This one would administer a fatal
blow to "the original serpent, the one called
Devil and Satan," and thus release mankind from
his wicked domination. (Genesis 3:15; Revelation
12:9) After making this statement of purpose,
Jehovah proceeded to make definite preparations
for the eventual administration of earth's affairs

11. (a) What statement of purpose did Jehovah make in Eden?
(b) What has God been doing since then?

under the promised "seed." This preparatory work would take time, as we shall see.

WHY HE DEALT SPECIFICALLY WITH ISRAEL

[12] Long before the nations of our present time came into existence, God selected one nation as his own people for hundreds of years. Why? In order to make a *living demonstration* of the operation of his righteous principles. That nation was made up of descendants of Abraham, a man who had displayed great faith in the Creator. To them Jehovah said: "It was not because of your being the most populous of all the peoples that Jehovah showed affection for you so that he chose you, for you were the least of all the peoples. But it was because of Jehovah's loving you, and because of his keeping the sworn statement that he had sworn to your forefathers."—Deuteronomy 7:7, 8; 2 Kings 13:23 [4 Kings 13:23, *Dy*].

[13] After delivering them from slavery in Egypt, Jehovah brought them to Mount Sinai and there offered to take them into covenant relationship with him. They replied: "All that Jehovah has spoken we are willing to do." (Exodus 19:8) Jehovah then proceeded to give them his regulations and judicial decisions. This set them apart from all other nations and provided detailed information for men concerning God's own righteous standards. (Deuteronomy 4:5-8) So, Israelite history provides a record of what happens when God's wise, righteous laws are either obeyed or disobeyed. At the same time, the history

12, 13. (a) Why did God select Israel and give his laws to just that one nation? (b) So, what can we learn from the history of Israel and from that of other nations?

of other nations provides a contrast, revealing the outcome to those who live without God's law.

[14] What about those other nations? They went their own way, choosing their own forms of government. Their people were not totally bereft of all goodness in their lives. They still had the faculty of conscience, and this at times moved them to act with humanitarian concern for their fellowman. (Romans 2:14; Acts 28:1, 2) But their inheritance of sin and their rejection of divine guidance caused them to pursue basically a self-seeking course. This led to cruel wars and depraved practices to satisfy their selfish passions. (Ephesians 4:17-19) God was not responsible for the woes that they brought on themselves. Their course of life was what they themselves chose. God did not interfere with them, except when their activities were in conflict with the outworking of his purposes. Yet, in his undeserved kindness, he allowed them to enjoy the sun and rain, the beauties of his creation and the fruitage of the earth.—Acts 14:16, 17.

[15] Nor did Jehovah shut these nations out from being among those who could eventually receive blessings by means of the promised Seed. Abraham was told that the Seed would be produced through his family line, and concerning the results of this, Jehovah said: "By means of your seed *all nations of the earth* will certainly bless themselves due to the fact that you have listened to my voice." (Genesis 22:18) So we see that, while Jehovah was dealing exclusively with Israel,

---

14. (a) Did God wrong the non-Israelite nations by not interfering in their affairs? (b) Yet, how did they benefit from God's undeserved kindness?
15. What arrangements for the eventual blessing of people of these nations was God working out?

he was impartially working out his purpose to bless the other nations later, although they were ignorant of that fact.—Acts 10:34, 35.

¹⁶ During the time that Jehovah was dealing with fleshly Israel, he provided numerous prophecies that would fill a vital need. They would enable men of faith to identify the promised Seed, Jehovah's Anointed One, when he eventually arrived. His family line—through the tribe of Judah and the house of David—was specified. (Genesis 49:10; Psalm 89:35, 36 [88:36, 37, *Dy*]) The place of his birth, Bethlehem, was named. (Micah 5:2) Centuries in advance, the very time when he, as a grown man, would be anointed, thus becoming the Messiah, was indicated. (Daniel 9:24-27) His priestly services on behalf of mankind were foreshadowed, as was the sacrifice of himself that he would offer in order to open the way for people of all nations to attain to the opportunity for eternal life when God's Judgment Day would arrive. (Hebrews 9:23-28) Thus, when the appointed time arrived, everything unmistakably identified Jesus Christ as the one whom Jehovah had sent forth as the Seed of promise, the one through whom blessings would eventually come to all mankind.—Galatians 3:16, 24; 2 Corinthians 1:19, 20.

THE PREPARING OF RULERS FOR MANKIND

¹⁷ Here was the one through whom God would grant peace to mankind. Before his birth his mother Mary had been told by an angel of God

16. (a) During all this time, what was God doing in connection with the promise about the Seed? (b) Who did that Seed of promise prove to be?
17. Through Jesus, what was God going to bring about, and how was this emphasized at the time of his birth?

that her son would be given an everlasting kingdom. Shepherds near Bethlehem were notified of his birth, and then they heard a multitude of the armies of heaven praising God and saying: "Glory in the heights above to God, and upon earth peace among men of goodwill."—Luke 1:31-33; 2:10-14.

[18] Consider the benefits of this future heavenly king's having lived on earth. As a man he came to know and understand the problems of mankind. He lived and worked with them, sharing their grief and personally suffering hardship. Under the most severe tests he proved his loyalty to Jehovah and his love of righteousness. All this was part of God's way of preparing him to be King over heaven and earth and High Priest to administer life-giving benefits to mankind. (Hebrews 1:9; 4:15; 5:8-10) Furthermore, by means of his own life laid down as a sacrifice, Jesus Christ opened the way for mankind to regain peaceful relations with God.—1 Peter 3:18.

[19] After his death, God raised him to life again and saw to it that there were over five hundred human witnesses to testify to the fact that this is what had actually happened. (1 Corinthians 15:3-8) Then, forty days later, with his disciples looking on, he ascended heavenward and disappeared from their sight. (Acts 1:9) From heaven he proceeded to exercise his kingship toward his own faithful followers, and the benefits of his rule made them stand out in contrast to the rest

18. (a) In what way did his experiences on earth prepare him for the offices of king and priest? (b) What effect did his death have on the gaining of peace?
19. (a) How do we know that Jesus was resurrected and ascended to heaven? (b) As to his kingship, what did he do after returning to heaven?

of mankind. But was it now the due time for him to receive kingly authority over the nations? No, for other matters in God's great program required attention.—Hebrews 10:12, 13.

[20] A major work had to be done earth wide. Prior to Jesus' death and resurrection, no Israelites had gone out as preachers to convert other nations—although any who desired to take up the worship of Jehovah could always receive blessings with Israel. (1 Kings 8:41-43 [3 Kings 8:41-43, *Dy*]) With the beginning of Christianity, however, a new work opened up. Jesus Christ himself first set the example in Israel. Then, while he was still with his disciples, before his ascension to heaven, he told them: "You will be witnesses of me both in Jerusalem and in all Judea and Samaria and to the most distant part of the earth." —Acts 1:8.

[21] Was world conversion the objective? No. Rather, as Jesus showed in an illustration concerning "the kingdom of the heavens," what would be accomplished during the period down into the "conclusion of the system of things" would be a gathering together of "the sons of the kingdom." Yes, the other members of the coming Kingdom government must be selected. (Matthew 13:24-30, 36-43) Anyone reading the Christian Greek Scriptures can readily see that, starting with Pentecost of 33 C.E., the hope held out to believers was of sharing with Jesus Christ in his Kingdom rule in heaven.—2 Timothy 2:12; Hebrews 3:1; 1 Peter 1:3, 4.

20. What new work had Jesus opened up for his disciples on earth?
21. Instead of world conversion, what was God accomplishing by means of that witnessing?

²² The selecting of these future corulers over mankind would take time. Why? For one thing, that hope, something more precious than the finest of gems, was to be extended to people of all nations. While many professed to lay hold of it, few truly proved to be faithful followers of God's Son. (Matthew 13:45, 46; 22:14) High standards were to be met. Christians have not lived as a national group apart from other people, as fleshly Israel did. As a result their faith and endurance have been severely tested. They have been as aliens in the world, advocating another way of life, one in harmony with God's righteous principles. (1 Peter 2:11, 12) To be approved, they must keep clean from the immoral and corrupt practices of the world around them. (1 Corinthians 6:9, 10) If they are really to be "sons of God," they must prove themselves to be "peaceable," not engaging in the wars of the nations and not retaliating when persecuted for their faith. (Matthew 5:9; 26:52; Romans 12:18, 19) It has been required that they demonstrate unwavering loyalty to rulership by God, refusing to be identified as advocates of the political governments of mankind, which the Bible refers to as 'beasts.' (Revelation 20:4, 6) Because of this, and because they have adhered to the name of Jesus Christ as God's anointed king, they have been "objects of hatred by all the nations." (Matthew 24:9) So, those who are to be the heavenly rulers of mankind along with Christ have not been hastily chosen.

---

22. (a) What qualities did God require in these prospective heirs of the heavenly kingdom? (b) So, was the choosing done hastily?

²³ The length of time taken is not because the number chosen was to be great. According to the Scriptures, God limited the number of this select administrative body under Jesus Christ to 144,000 persons. (Revelation 14:1-3) But God has chosen them carefully. They have been taken "out of every tribe and tongue and people and nation." (Revelation 5:9, 10) Among them are people from all walks of life, men and women, persons who have shared all the varied problems of mankind. In the course of their putting on the new Christian personality, there is simply no problem that some of them have not faced and overcome. (Ephesians 4:22-24; 1 Corinthians 10:13) How glad we can be for this, since it gives us the assurance that they will be sympathetic and merciful kings and priests, able to help men and women of all kinds, assisting them to lay hold of God's provision for eternal life.

²⁴ What of mankind outside this Christian congregation? During all this time, God was not interfering with the governmental affairs of the world. He let men go in the way that they chose. Of course, millions of persons lived and died, many of them never hearing about the Bible or the kingdom of God. Yet *God had not forgotten them*. He was preparing for the time concerning which the apostle Paul spoke to a Roman governor of his day, saying: "I have hope toward God . . . that there is going to be a resurrection of both the righteous and the unrighteous." (Acts 24:15) Then, under the most favorable conditions, in

23. (a) How many are to be in that heavenly administrative body with Christ? (b) From among whom have they been selected, and why?

24. What about the millions of other persons who lived and died during this time, many of them ignorant of the Bible?

God's new order, they would be given opportunity to learn Jehovah's ways and to decide what stand they personally would take on the issue of universal sovereignty. Proving themselves to be lovers of righteousness, they could live forever.

AS "THE END" DRAWS NEAR

[25] Before the incoming of that new order, thrilling events were to occur. The Bible foretold a momentous change in world affairs. Jesus Christ would be enthroned as king, not merely to rule over his own disciples, but with authority to take action toward the whole world. At this time the proclamation would be made in heaven: "The kingdom of the world did become the kingdom of our Lord and of his Christ, and he will rule as king forever and ever." (Revelation 11:15) Authorized by God to act against his enemies, he would first move against "the ruler of the world" himself, Satan the Devil, and his demons. (John 14:30) These wicked forces would be hurled down from the heavens, and confined to the vicinity of the earth. What would be the result?

[26] The prophetic description of this event, as found in Revelation, records a voice out of heaven as saying: "On this account be glad, you heavens and you who reside in them! Woe for the earth and for the sea, because the Devil has come down to you, having great anger, knowing he has a short period of time." (Revelation 12:12) Unprecedented turmoil would take place among the nations, but the end would not come at once.

25, 26. (a) In due time, what further authority would Christ be given, and against whom would he take action? (b) How would this affect conditions on the earth?

²⁷ This would be the time when a great separating work would be done. Under the direction of Jesus Christ from his heavenly throne, his faithful followers would press the preaching of "this good news of the kingdom" into all the inhabited earth for a witness to all nations. (Matthew 24:14; 25:31-33) People everywhere would be given the opportunity to show their attitude toward divine rulership. With this accomplished, as Jesus explained, "then the end will come." It will be a "great tribulation such as has not occurred since the world's beginning until now, no, nor will occur again." (Matthew 24:21) Never again will men ask, What has God been doing? The only ones to survive will be those who cared enough to find out what he was doing and to bring their lives into harmony with his requirements before the world destruction arrived.

²⁸ But when are these things to take place? When is Christ given power to rule as king and to proceed with the separating of the people of all nations? The facts show that these are things that God has done in the twentieth century. Christ is already on his heavenly throne and the separating work is now nearing its completion. The time left in which you can identify yourself as being on Jehovah's side of the issue of universal sovereignty is very short. The "great tribulation" is near at hand! A careful examination of Bible prophecy in the light of recent history proves this to be true. We urge you to consider it carefully.

---

27. (a) As "the end" would draw near, what great separating work would take place, and how? (b) How great will the foretold world destruction be?
28. (a) When do the enthronement of Christ and the dividing of people of all nations take place? (b) So, what is it urgent for us individually to do?

CHAPTER 7

When Will the Foretold World Destruction Come?

WHAT a relief it would be to see war, crime and pollution of the earth brought to an end! How pleasant to live under a truly righteous administration, where there could be the enjoyment of full security for oneself and one's family! The Bible shows that God will make these things a reality. But when?

² With reference to the world destruction that clears the way for God's righteous new order, an apostle of Jesus Christ wrote: "Jehovah's day is coming exactly as a thief in the night." Then, addressing himself to persons who study and heed God's Word, he adds: "But you, brothers, you are not in darkness, so that that day should overtake you as it would thieves." (1 Thessalonians 5:2, 4) Those who fail to heed the warning will be taken by surprise. When "Jehovah's day" arrives, they will be like an animal caught suddenly in a snare from which it cannot escape. But that does not have to be your experience. As the scripture states, there are people who "are not in darkness." This is not because of any wisdom originating with them. Rather, it is because they study and take to heart God's Word. What does that Word say regarding our day? —Luke 21:34-36.

1. What grand purpose does God have for mankind?
2. (a) When "Jehovah's day" comes, who will be caught by surprise? (b) How can we avoid having that happen to us?

[3] It describes events of this twentieth century. But it did this some two thousand years in advance! While many of the events themselves are common knowledge, only the Bible points out their full significance.

[4] Among the information contained in the Bible regarding our day is the following: (1) Identification of a *specific year* as the time when God would give rulership over the "kingdom of mankind" to "the one whom he wants to." (2) Listing of *significant events* that would take place during the period known as "the conclusion of the system of things." (3) Indication as to the *length of time* from the beginning of "the conclusion of the system of things" until the foretold world destruction arrives. (4) Mention of a striking development in world affairs as *a final signal* that world destruction is about to begin. Let us examine these points one at a time.

THE MARKED YEAR—1914 C.E.

[5] The year 1914 C.E. is marked by Bible prophecy as a time when major events in the heavens would have far-reaching effects on human affairs. As far back as 1876 Jehovah's witnesses (then known as "Bible Students") realized that fact and gave it wide publicity. You can examine the details for yourself in your own Bible.

[6] Open your Bible to Daniel chapter 4. There you will find a prophecy that reveals God's pur-

3, 4. (a) Where is the full significance of the events of the twentieth century explained? (b) What four main points set out in Bible prophecy are we going to examine here?
5. At how early a date did Jehovah's witnesses realize that the Bible pointed to 1914 C.E. as a significant year?
6. (a) Open your Bible to Daniel chapter 4, and from verses 3 and 17 show what is being discussed there. (b) Who is the one to whom Jehovah gives the "kingdom"?

pose as to exercising his sovereignty over the earth. The purpose of that prophecy is stated as being "that people living may know that the Most High is Ruler in the kingdom of mankind and that to the one whom he wants to, he gives it." (Verses 3, 17) We know that this "one" to whom the Most High chooses to give the "kingdom" is Christ Jesus. The last book of the Bible tells of the time that "the kingdom of the world" is given to Christ as heavenly king. (Revelation 11:15; 12:10) This means, then, that the prophecy of Daniel deals with the time when the Most High God would intervene in human affairs by conferring "the kingdom of the world" on his own Son, Jesus Christ. When does the prophecy show that would be?

⁷ The prophetic dream recorded by Daniel mentions an immense tree that was chopped down and banded with iron and copper until "seven times" passed over it. During that time, it was said, "the heart of a beast" would be given to it. (Daniel 4:10-17) What did this mean? God caused his own prophet Daniel to explain: Nebuchadnezzar, the king of Babylon, was to be removed from his throne and driven from among men to live as a beast. After seven years the king's sanity returned, he acknowledged the superiority of God's rulership, and he himself was restored to his throne. (Daniel 4:20-37) All this had a greater meaning, however, and for that reason it is recorded in the Bible.

⁸ This greater meaning relates to a rulership

7. What is the gist of the prophetic dream in Daniel chapter 4, and how did it apply to King Nebuchadnezzar?
8. (a) The greater meaning of the prophecy relates to what kingdom? (b) In this greater fulfillment, what is represented by the cutting down of the tree, and how was 'the heart of a beast given to it'?

from which all living things on earth would benefit. From it, as the prophecy says, there would be "food for all," and protection for even the animals and birds. (Daniel 4:12; compare Matthew 13:31, 32.) The only rulership that truly can provide this is the kingdom of God. For centuries the righteous principles of that kingship were demonstrated by means of the government of Judah, with its king of the royal line of David in Jerusalem. But because of their unfaithfulness, Jehovah let them be conquered by the Babylonian king Nebuchadnezzar. It was as if the immense tree seen in the dream had been cut down and bands put around the stump. Gentile governments then exercised world domination, and Babylon, ruled by Nebuchadnezzar, was most prominent. These Gentile kingdoms are represented in the Bible by "beasts." (Daniel 8:1-8, 20-22) So, what was taking place in the affairs of government was as an angel from heaven had announced: "Let the heart of a beast be given to it, and let seven times pass over it." (Daniel 4:16) Eventually, however, those "seven times" would expire, the 'bands' would be removed, and the "tree" would grow as world domination began to be exercised by the one to whom Jehovah said that he would give "the kingdom of the world."

⁹ How long would those "seven times" prove to be? They were far more than seven literal years, because hundreds of years later Jesus Christ indicated that they had not yet expired. In the first century of our Common Era, he made

9, 10. (a) In figuring the length of the "seven times," how long does each 'time' prove to be? How does the Bible indicate this? (b) When did the "seven times" begin, how many years do they cover, and when do they end?

mention of them as "the appointed times of the nations," that is, the Gentile nations, which had held world domination since Babylon's conquest of Jerusalem in 607 B.C.E.—Luke 21:24.

[10] Notice for yourself how the Bible refers to prophetic "times." Revelation 11:2, 3 shows that 1,260 days comprise forty-two months, or three and a half years. Revelation 12:6, 14 mentions the same number of days (1,260) but refers to them as "a time and times and half a time," or three and a half "times." Each of those "times," then, must be 360 days ($3\frac{1}{2} \times 360 = 1{,}260$). Furthermore, each day of the prophetic "times" of Daniel's prophecy stands for a whole year, according to the rule, "A day for a year," as recorded under inspiration by two separate prophets of God. (Numbers 14:34; Ezekiel 4:6) With this established, it is not difficult to determine that "seven times" (7×360) is 2,520 years. Counting from autumn of 607 B.C.E., when the typical kingdom of God in Judah was brought low by Babylon, 2,520 years bring us to the autumn of 1914 C.E. ($606\frac{1}{4} + 1913\frac{3}{4} = 2{,}520$) as the time when "the kingdom of the world" was due to be entrusted to Jesus Christ on his heavenly throne.

[11] After realizing that the Bible did indeed point to the year 1914 C.E., Jehovah's witnesses had to wait for several decades before they saw the outcome. Early in the year 1914 the peacefulness of the world situation made it appear to many persons, including world leaders, that nothing was going to happen. But before the summer was over, the world had been plunged into a war that was without precedent in all

---

11. What do historians say as to the significance of the year 1914?

human history. Concerning the events of that year, Oxford historian A. L. Rowse has written:

"If ever there was a year that marked the end of an era and the beginning of another, it was 1914. That year brought to an end the old world with its sense of security and began the modern age, characteristic of which is the insecurity that is our daily portion."[23]

And a report on a book on the life of British statesman Winston Churchill likewise notes:

"The shot which was fired on June 28, 1914, in Sarajevo, had shattered the world of security and creative reason . . . The world has never been the same place since. . . . It was a turning point, and the wonderful, calm, attractive world of yesterday had vanished, never again to appear."—Review of the book *Winston S. Churchill*, Vol. 2, by Randolph Churchill.[24]

That year, marked by Bible prophecy about two and a half millenniums earlier, indeed proved to be a turning point in history. Its true significance became even more clear as further events began to unfold.

[12] It may at first seem strange that the time when Christ was to take his throne to rule over the world of mankind would be marked by unprecedented war on earth. But do not forget that "the ruler of the world" of mankind alienated from God is Satan the Devil. (John 14:30) He did not want to see the newborn kingdom of God in the hands of Christ take over the control of earth's affairs. Evidently in an endeavor to divert the attention of men from that event of universal importance, he maneuvered them into a war to uphold their own claims to sovereignty. Furthermore, as the Bible shows, when the King-

---

12. What was the reason for the great upheaval in human affairs in 1914 and thereafter?

dom was brought to birth and became fully operative, Satan and his demons were ready to devour the newborn government. What was the result? "War broke out in heaven." "Down the great dragon was hurled, the original serpent, the one called Devil and Satan, who is misleading the entire inhabited earth; he was hurled down to the earth, and his angels were hurled down with him." Satan knew that he had remaining only "a short period of time." His anger was great. (Revelation 12:3-12) What would be the result? Nineteen centuries in advance the Bible provided an accurate description.

EVENTS WITH SPECIAL SIGNIFICANCE

[13] Back in the year 33 C.E. Jesus had described in detail 'the sign of his presence and of the conclusion of the system of things.' This is recorded in the Bible in Matthew chapters 24 and 25, Mark 13 and Luke 21. While with a group of his disciples in Jerusalem, Jesus had foretold the destruction of the magnificent temple standing there. Shortly thereafter, when he sat down on a hillside outside the city, his disciples asked for further information, saying: "Tell us, When will these things be, and what will be the sign of your presence and of the conclusion of the system of things?"—Matthew 24:1-3.

[14] After warning them not to be misled by impostors who, in an endeavor to get followers, would claim to be Christ, he said in answer: "You are going to hear of wars and reports of wars; see that you are not terrified. For these

---

13. What led up to Jesus' stating the 'sign of his presence and of the conclusion of the system of things'?
14. Name some of the significant events that Jesus included in "the sign."

things must take place, but the end is not yet [or, does not occur immediately]. For nation will rise against nation and kingdom against kingdom, and there will be food shortages and earthquakes in one place after another. All these things are a beginning of pangs of distress." As Luke 21:11 shows, he also made mention of 'pestilences in one place after another.' He warned of "the increasing of lawlessness," and because of this, he said, "the love of the greater number will cool off." And, significantly, he foretold: "This good news of the kingdom will be preached in all the inhabited earth for a witness to all the nations; and then the end will come."—Matthew 24:4-14.

¹⁵ But the question may be asked: 'Were not some of these prophecies fulfilled before the destruction of Jerusalem by the Romans in the year 70 C.E.?' Yes, some of them were; but more was to come, as the prophecies themselves show. Jesus was answering a question that was of immediate concern to his disciples, but, in so doing, he used the opportunity to provide long-range information about matters of even greater importance. He told them that he was also speaking about the time when "the Son of man" would come "with power and great glory" and that what he was saying had reference to the coming of "the kingdom of God."—Luke 21:27, 31.

¹⁶ These things did not take place by the time of Jerusalem's destruction in 70 C.E. The last book of the Bible, the Revelation, written shortly before the end of the first century, showed that these events in relation to the Kingdom were

15, 16. (a) Did any of those things happen before Jerusalem was destroyed in 70 C.E.? (b) How do we know that there must also be another, even more important, fulfillment?

yet future. (Revelation 1:1; 11:15-18; 12:3-12) In symbolic language the book of Revelation also showed that the war, food shortage, and pestilence that Jesus had foretold would have a future fulfillment, on an unusual scale, at the time when Christ would begin and complete his conquest of all opposers of God's kingdom. (Revelation 6:1-8) But the fact that major portions of Jesus' prophecy to his disciples did have a fulfillment in the first century stamped it as truthful, and this gives sound reason for confidence in the fulfillment of everything else contained in that prophecy.

[17] Have these prophecies found that greater, complete fulfillment in this twentieth century? To uninformed persons who are less than seventy years of age, conditions that surround them in the world today may not seem particularly significant. Not remembering a time when life was much different, they may feel that perhaps our times are quite 'normal.' But older persons, as also those who are informed on matters of history, know that this is not the case. Thus, concerning the events that broke upon the world in the year 1914 C.E., a history textbook used in Swiss schools stated:

> "Only fifteen countries did not get involved in the war . . . But among them there was no great country that would have had the power to act as mediator. This had never occurred in world history; no war had ever had such dimensions. The prophecy of the Holy Bible: 'Nation will rise up against nation and kingdom against kingdom,' was literally fulfilled."—*Schweizergeschichte vom Dreiländerbund bis zum Völkerbund,* by Gustav Wiget.[25]

17. Are the conditions in the world today really very different from what they were before 1914?

[18] But it was not just 'nation rising against nation and kingdom against kingdom' that Jesus had stated to be "the sign." Using an illustration, he said: "Note the fig tree and all the other trees: When they are already in the bud, by observing it you know for yourselves that now the summer is near. In this way you also, when you see these things occurring, know that the kingdom of God is near. Truly I say to you, This generation will by no means pass away until all things occur." (Luke 21:29-32) If you were to see just one tree putting forth leaves out of season, you would not be fooled into thinking that summer was at hand. But when you see *all* the trees budding, you know what it means. Likewise, Jesus foretold that his "presence" and "the conclusion of the system of things" would be marked, not just by war, but by a number of things all taking place in one generation.

[19] Have those things come to pass? Examine the accompanying chart that bears the heading "What Will Be the Sign?" As you do so, you may recall reading about wars of earlier centuries. But it is evident that World War I stands out from all the others as distinctive, as a turning point in history. You may recall, also, that notable food shortages, pestilences, earthquakes or times of lawlessness have been reported by historians as taking place before 1914. Yet, at no other time in history have all these things come on one generation in such overwhelming measure. The other features of "the sign" as recorded by the Gospel

18. Why would we be wrong if we were to conclude that widespread war was all there was to "the sign"?
19. (a) As shown on the accompanying chart, how have the various features of "the sign" been fulfilled since 1914? (b) Why do earlier wars, food shortages, earthquakes, and so forth, not constitute "the sign" of which Jesus spoke?

"What Will Be the Sign?"

"NATION WILL RISE AGAINST NATION" —

"World War I ushered in the century of Total War, of—in the first full sense of the term—global war. . . . Never before 1914-1918 had a war . . . covered so large a part of the earth. . . . Never had the slaughter been so comprehensive and indiscriminate."—"World War I," by H. Baldwin.

World War I killed over 9 million combatants, and millions more of civilians.

World War II left 55 million dead.

Within about two decades after World War II, there were more than 300 further coups, uprisings, rebellions world wide.

"THERE WILL BE FOOD SHORTAGES" —

Food shortages ravaged many lands after World War I, and again after World War II.

Despite years of unprecedented scientific advance, in 1967, it was reported, 10,000 were dying every day, 3,500,000 every year due to malnutrition.

"In the 1970's the world will undergo famines —hundreds of millions of people are going to starve to death in spite of any crash programs embarked upon now."—"The Population Bomb," by Dr. Paul Ehrlich.

"PESTILENCES" —

No recorded pestilence has ever equaled that of the Spanish influenza of 1918-1919. It struck at least 500 million persons; over 20 million died.

Today, medical research has not been able to prevent heart disease from reaching epidemic proportions; cancer is common. The number of cases of venereal disease has skyrocketed.

"EARTHQUAKES" IN MANY PLACES —

In 1915 at Avezzano, Italy, 29,970 died in an earthquake; 180,000 in China in 1920; 143,000 in Japan in 1923; 60,000 in India in 1935. The 1960's saw great quakes in Iran, Chile, Morocco, Yugoslavia, Libya, El Salvador, Russia, Colombia, France, Indonesia and Turkey, among others. In 1970 an earthquake killed 70,000 in Peru, and over 12,000 died in Nicaragua in 1972.

"INCREASING OF LAWLESSNESS" —

You know the facts. Your own life has been affected. In your community, what has been happening in the schools? Is there illegal use of drugs in your area? What about dishonesty in business? How safe do you feel on the streets at night?

So widespread is the "crime crisis" that, in 1972, the Secretary-General of the United Nations called for international action.

The lawlessness is not only as regards human law, but even more so is the law of God ignored.

GOD'S KINGDOM PREACHED WORLD WIDE —

This work is regularly being done in 208 lands.

During just the past thirty years, 3,676,343,869 hours have been devoted by Jehovah's Christian witnesses to public preaching of this message. In that same period they published, in over 160 languages, more than 5 billion pieces of literature pointing to God's kingdom as man's only hope.

Of what are these things "the sign"? That we are living now in "the conclusion of the system of things." That Christ has taken his heavenly throne, and is separating out from people of all nations those who truly do the will of God. That the "great tribulation" is very near!

(For further details, read Matthew chapters 24, 25, Mark 13 and Luke 21.)

writers are also clearly in evidence. In all honesty, if the events since 1914 do not fulfill the sign, what more is required? Without a doubt, we live in the generation of which Jesus spoke.

[20] The appearance of these features of "the sign" did not mean that God's kingdom would immediately clean all wickedness out of the earth. As Jesus foretold, "all these things are *a beginning* of pangs of distress." (Matthew 24:8) Others were to follow. In regard to what developed, the *World Book Encyclopedia* states: "World War I and its aftermath led to the greatest economic depression in history during the early 1930's. The consequences of the war and the problems of adjustment to peace led to unrest in almost every nation."[26] A few years later World War II erupted, many times more horrible than the first. Since then, disregard for life and property has grown, and fear of crime has become part of everyday life. Morals have been shoved aside. The "population explosion" is posing problems to which leaders say they have no real solution. Pollution of the environment is spoiling the quality of life and threatening to wipe it out. As a result, a report on a United Nations Conference on the Human Environment declared that the human family stands at the threshold of "a crisis more sudden, more global, more inescapable, and more bewildering than any ever encountered by the human species."[27]

[21] When was it that these "pangs of distress" began? The London *Star* observed: "Some historian in the next century may well conclude that the day the world went mad was . . . [in] 1914."[28] As we have already seen, that year,

20, 21. How did the events associated with World War I prove to be only "a beginning of pangs of distress," as Jesus foretold?

1914 C.E., had long in advance been marked by Bible prophecy.

NOTEWORTHY RELIGIOUS DEVELOPMENTS

[22] Among the significant events that Jesus listed as due to occur during the "conclusion of the system of things" were the following: "Many false prophets will arise and mislead many; and because of the increasing of lawlessness the love of the greater number will cool off." (Matthew 24:11, 12) It should be noted that Jesus associated the increased lawlessness and the cooling off of love with the influence of false prophets, that is, religious teachers who falsely claim to speak for God. Earlier in this book evidence was presented showing that the clergy of Christendom have blessed the wars of the nations, advocated the idea that Bible standards of morality are out-of-date and labeled portions of the Bible as "myth." What has been the result? A 'cooling off' in love for God and concern about his law. This has been a major factor in the general breakdown in morality, including disregard for authority and the lack of concern for one's fellowman.—2 Timothy 3:1-5.

[23] Because of the conditions that have developed, people by the thousands are leaving the religious organizations of Christendom. Some are turning to the Bible and are conforming their lives to its ways. Others are merely withdrawing in disappointment and disgust, seeing that the churches are failing to provide genuine spiritual help. Many are becoming enemies of the churches.

---

22. (a) With what did Jesus associate his forecast of increased lawlessness and the cooling off of love? (b) How have the teachings of the clergy of Christendom contributed to this situation? 23, 24. As a result, what has been happening to the churches in recent years?

[24] That is why the New York *Post* could say: "The area in which the old order seems to be reeling past us with the speed of light is religion."[29] And the New York *Times* reported: "Institutional religion is on the way out, a German expert on sociology of religion said."[30] The Vatican weekly *L'Osservatore Della Domenica* admitted that the Roman Catholic Church in the United States was being shaken by a "tremendous earthquake."[31] It said that nearly every day "some new disaster" was befalling the church, such as priests deserting, nuns quitting and Catholic schools and seminaries closing. In all the religions of Christendom, fewer young men are entering the seminaries, religious schools are closing their doors, and a great number of religious magazines have ceased publication. The churches in general are finding their attendances growing smaller. Many church buildings are up for sale.

[25] By contrast with this, the Bible indicates that a "great crowd" out of all nations would be drawn to true worship in this time of the end. (Revelation 7:9, 10, 14) This gathering together of worshipers of the true God is done under the direction of Christ Jesus. He foretold that, when he returned "in his glory," he would give attention to people of all the nations, separating them one from another with a view to their preservation through the "great tribulation" or their eternal destruction. (Matthew 25: 31-33) On what basis are they separated? Jesus

---

25. (a) In contrast, what does the Bible indicate would be taking place in regard to true worship in this time? (b) Under whose direction is this gathering of worshipers of the true God done, and on what basis? (c) So, with what issue are people of all nations being confronted?

said that it would be on the basis of how they treated his spiritual "brothers" here on earth. Why? Because these are representatives of God's kingdom in the hands of Jesus Christ. In obedience to him, the message they preach is "this good news of the kingdom." And they are doing so "in all the inhabited earth for a witness to all the nations." (Matthew 24:14) This news of the Kingdom confronts the people of all nations with the issue of universal sovereignty. Are they for rulership by God? Or, in harmony with Satan's urging in Eden, do they want independent rulership by men? Jehovah God through his Son gives people the opportunity to choose.

[26] A worldwide witness has been given. In 208 lands Jehovah's Christian witnesses visit people in their homes and offer to study the Bible with any family or individual, free of charge. The publications they use to announce God's kingdom are among the most widely circulated in the earth, available in over 160 languages.

[27] Already this separating work has been proceeding for many years. It is now very near its conclusion. According to God's Word, those who have deliberately rejected his Kingdom rule, as well as those who indifferently pass up the opportunity to learn of him, will then be cut off in everlasting destruction. (Matthew 25:34, 41, 46; 2 Thessalonians 1:6-9) For others who willingly and gladly identify themselves as genuine supporters of God's kingdom, this will mark a time of grand relief. How soon, then, does the Bible indicate that this expression of judgment will come?

26, 27. (a) To what extent has this witness work already been done? (b) Why is one's response to the Kingdom message a serious matter?

"THIS GENERATION WILL BY NO MEANS PASS AWAY"

[28] As to "that day and hour," Jesus said, "nobody knows, neither the angels of the heavens nor the Son, but only the Father." (Matthew 24:36) But Jesus did give a helpful time indicator when he said: "This generation will by no means pass away until all these things occur." (Matthew 24:34) All what things? All the various features of "the sign" about which he was speaking, as well as the "great tribulation," which he had also mentioned. For these things to take place within a generation would mean that persons who were on hand to observe what happened in 1914 C.E., at the beginning of the "conclusion of the system of things," would still have to be alive at the end of this period, when the "great tribulation" strikes. Those who remember the events of 1914 are getting up in years now. Many of their number have already died. But, Jesus assures us, within "this generation," before they have all died, destruction of this wicked system of things will come.

[29] How patient God has been in allowing this time period! During this generation, for the first time in history, one problem after another has reached gigantic proportions—war, pollution, overpopulation and more. Any one of them could bring complete ruin. By letting the evidence pile up, God has made it easier for humans to realize that rule by man holds no real solution. At the same time, by means of the preaching of the "good news of the kingdom," he has helped

---

28. How soon did Jesus say the foretold world destruction would come?
29. By allowing events since 1914 to develop to the point that they have, how has God made it easier for humans to make the right decision?

honest-hearted ones to recognize that the kingdom of God is the only hope for true peace and security and to identify themselves on his side of the great issue.

[30] There is yet one more definite event to come that serves as an *unmistakable signal* that world destruction is imminent. This signal was pointed to by the apostle Paul when he wrote: "Jehovah's day is coming exactly as a thief in the night. Whenever it is that they are saying: 'Peace and security!' then sudden destruction is to be instantly upon them . . . and they will by no means escape."—1 Thessalonians 5:2, 3; Luke 21:34, 35.

[31] The political leaders of the world know that, if they were to get involved in nuclear war, no one could win. It would result in virtual extinction. Furthermore, the grave problems involving pollution of the environment, the "population explosion" and other domestic problems demand attention and money. So, they have worked hard to try to achieve a relaxation of the strained international relations. Of course, their negotiations are not making any real changes in the people so that they love one another. They are not putting a stop to crime, or eliminating disease and death. Yet the prophecy shows that the time will come when they will declare that "peace and security" at last exist. When that occurs, then "sudden destruction" will come "instantly" upon those misleaders of mankind, along with all who put their trust in them.

[32] But there will be survivors. Will you be among them?

---

30. What final signal of the closeness of world destruction does the Bible specify?
31, 32. (a) Will the "peace and security" that political rulers proclaim be genuine? (b) Why would it be dangerous to be misled by it?

CHAPTER 8

Who Will the Survivors Be?

SURVIVAL of the coming world destruction will not be a matter of chance, as so often happens in human wars. It will not be determined by the part of the earth in which one lives. Nor will it result from one's hurrying to some bomb shelter or other refuge at the sound of a warning siren. Survival will depend on God's mercy along with one's deliberate choice made before the foretold "great tribulation" begins. How can you make the choice that will place you among those surviving to life in a peaceful new order?

THE PROPHETIC PATTERN OF THE PAST

² The Bible not only foretells that persons will survive the coming world destruction. It also sets out a pattern enabling us to know what kind of persons they will be. Since God makes possible the survival, rightly he sets the terms.

³ God will wisely and justly see to it that those surviving the coming "great tribulation" are persons who will do good in his new order, not work to its harm. He will preserve only those who love righteousness. If he did otherwise, letting unrighteous persons survive, there would be no peace and security. The homes and personal

---

1. Upon what will one's survival into God's peaceful new order depend?
2. Who sets the terms for survival, and where are these found?
3. For there to be peace and security, why is it necessary for evildoers to be cut off?

safety of upright people would still be endangered. But his inspired Word promises: "Evildoers themselves will be cut off, but those hoping in Jehovah are the ones that will possess the earth. And just a little while longer, and the wicked one will be no more . . . But the meek ones themselves will possess the earth." Only by God's applying to its full extent the standard set forth here at Psalm 37:9-11 [36:9-11, *Dy*] will survivors be able to "find their exquisite delight in the abundance of peace," as is further promised in this scripture. How God will do this is seen in the record of past occasions when men's wickedness obliged God to bring destruction.

PAST EXAMPLES OF SURVIVAL

4 In the city of Rome today there still stands an arch from the first century of the Common Era, known as the Arch of Titus. On its interior walls is depicted the carrying away of items from the temple in Jerusalem after the destruction of that city in 70 C.E. That destruction is a historical fact. Equally historical is the fact that, decades before that destruction, Jesus Christ had foretold both its coming and how persons could survive it.

5 The Jewish people had turned away from God; they were following men and the religious traditions of men, not God and his Word. (Matthew 15:3-9) They put their faith in human political rulers and not in God's promised kingdom. (John 19:15) They went so far as to reject

4-6. (a) What testifies that the destruction of Jerusalem in 70 C.E. is a historical fact? (b) Why did the destruction come? (c) What made it possible for the disciples of Jesus Christ to escape?

and even fight against the truth that God's Son and his apostles proclaimed. Christ Jesus warned of the consequences to which such a course would inevitably lead.—Matthew 23:37, 38; 24:1, 2.

⁶ The results were exactly as foretold in the Bible. In the year 66 C.E. the Jews revolted against Rome. An initial attack on Jerusalem by the Romans was followed by their unexpected retreat. This was the signal and opportunity for those believing God's Word to do what his Son had said: Flee—get out of the doomed city and out of the whole province of Judea, no matter what one might have to leave behind. Genuine disciples of Jesus Christ did just that. Then, in the year 70 C.E., the Romans returned and, after a siege, destroyed Jerusalem. An eyewitness, Jewish historian Josephus, claims that 1,100,000 persons in Jerusalem died by famine, disease, civil strife or the Roman sword. Yet those Christians who took positive action, demonstrating faith by obedience, escaped that destruction. —Luke 19:28, 41-44; 21:20-24; Matthew 24:15-18.

⁷ A similar situation had prevailed nearly seven centuries earlier. At that time Jehovah God allowed Babylonian forces under King Nebuchadnezzar (II) to wreck the Israelite nation. That destruction, too, is a matter of history. For years before, God through his prophets had warned the apostate people that their course was leading to disaster. "Turn back, turn back from your bad ways, for why is it that you should die?" was God's call to them. (Ezekiel 33:11) The majority

---

7. What did persons need to do to survive when Babylon wrecked the Israelite nation?

put no faith in the warning sounded. Even when
Jerusalem came under siege by Babylon's forces,
those Israelites still kept hoping that no destruction would come. Nevertheless, it took place as
foretold. Yet God fulfilled his promise of preservation to those who demonstrated by obedience
their faith in him.—Jeremiah 39:15-18; Zephaniah 2:2, 3 [Sophonias 2:2, 3, *Dy*].

⁸ Farther back in human history, we find the
earliest expression of the divine pattern for survival. It involves, not a national destruction, but
a world destruction, and that too is a historical
fact. This came in the global flood occurring during the years 2370/2369 B.C.E., in the days of
Noah. Of the conditions prevailing before that
world destruction, the historical account reads:
"Consequently Jehovah saw that the badness of
man was abundant in the earth and every inclination of the thoughts of his heart was only
bad all the time. And the earth came to be ruined
in the sight of the true God and the earth became filled with violence."—Genesis 6:5, 11.

⁹ The wickedness and violence obliged God to
act. On earth only Noah and his family showed
faith and obedience. Out of mercy to them and
to preserve justice and righteousness on earth,
Jehovah God did "not hold back from punishing
an ancient world . . . of ungodly people." The
result was that "the world of that time suffered
destruction when it was deluged with water."
—2 Peter 2:5; 3:5-7.

¹⁰ Yet Noah and his family survived. Why?

8-10. (a) Why did Jehovah bring a world destruction in the days
of Noah? (b) Why were Noah and his family spared?

First, Noah and his family did not go along with that "world of ungodly people" in their unrighteousness. They did not let themselves become so engrossed with the ordinary things of life, eating, drinking and marriage, that they became insensitive to God's will or deaf to his warning. Noah 'walked with God' in righteousness. This was not just a negative thing. He and his family did not merely refrain from doing bad acts. They took positive action; they *did things*, right acts. They really believed what God said, and showed it by obediently building a chestlike, three-story ark over four hundred feet in length, according to divine specifications. Noah was also "a preacher of righteousness," speaking out God's purposes, advocating the way of righteousness.—Genesis 6:9, 13-16; Matthew 24:37-39; Hebrews 11:7.

[11] These eight persons survived because of faith and works of faith. Since God's own Son and his apostles refer to that world destruction as prophetic of what faces people in this "time of the end," it is clear that we too must disassociate ourselves from the wrong course of the world of mankind today, which is every bit as ungodly as that in Noah's day. We too must work in harmony with God's will. We cannot simply be guided by our own standards and expect to survive. God's Word says: "There exists a way that is upright before a man, but the ways of death are the end of it afterward." (Proverbs 16:25) Nor will any superficial appearance of righteousness bring survival. For Jehovah God sees what the heart is.—Proverbs 24:12; Luke 16:15.

---

11. As indicated by these warning examples, what must we do if we are to survive the coming world destruction?

WHAT JEHOVAH LOOKS FOR
IN HUMAN HEARTS

[12] There are many people who are unhappy with present conditions. They show this by their complaints, demonstrations, strikes and, in some lands, by violent revolt. Many resent high taxation and the soaring cost of living. In many areas they bemoan the danger of crime. Fear makes them want a change. But, is this enough to assure their survival into God's new order? No, it is not. Why not?

[13] Because one could be unhappy over these conditions and yet be selfish. He might even approve of certain forms of dishonesty and immorality—just as long as he himself did not suffer. When a person gets a knowledge of the Bible, however, he can see that these bad conditions are but the outward evidences of the real sickness of this world. He discerns that behind these symptoms is disrespect for right principles and even for God himself, a lack of concern about knowing and doing Jehovah God's will and observing his righteous standards. Rather than being primarily upset and grieved because they are not getting certain material things or certain social rights, or because of the danger from crime, pollution and the threat of war, right-hearted persons are *especially* grieved at seeing humankind defaming God's name by their corrupt course. And they grieve that *others,* not just themselves, suffer so much as a result.

[14] To be among the survivors of the coming

12, 13. (a) What causes many people to want a change to better conditions? (b) Why is this not enough to assure their survival into God's new order? (c) To be among the survivors, what must motivate our grief over present bad conditions?
14. Who were the ones 'marked' for survival at the time of Jerusalem's destruction by Babylon?

world destruction, we must be like those whom
God spared when he permitted the armies of
Babylon to destroy Jerusalem. These persons
marked for survival were described as "sighing
and groaning over all the detestable things" that
were being done in the midst of the city. (Ezekiel
9:4) Conditions were very bad there; the poor
were being oppressed, some even held in slavery
illegally by their countrymen. (Jeremiah 34:
13-16) Jerusalem and the kingdom of Judah had
become even worse than had the northern kingdom of Israel and its capital, Samaria, of which
the prophet Hosea had earlier written: "There
are the pronouncing of curses and practicing of
deception and murdering and stealing . . . and
acts of bloodshed have touched other acts of
bloodshed." (Hosea 4:2; Ezekiel 16:2, 51) Only
those who felt grieved at heart because of such
unrighteousness and the disrespect it showed
for God were 'marked' for survival.—Ezekiel
9:2, 4-6.

¹⁵ There are many persons today who would
like to enjoy life in peace, with freedom from
fear and in prosperous, comfortable conditions.
But they do not want to change their way of life
by learning what God's Word says and by following its pattern for right living. They really
do not have a love of righteousness or sincerely
care about their fellowmen. Since God's new order
will produce a new earthly society in which "righteousness is to dwell," the good news about it
will have an appealing flavor only to those who
love righteousness; others feel condemned by it.
—2 Peter 3:13; 2 Corinthians 2:14-17.

---

15. What holds some persons back from making the changes
needed in order to be survivors of the coming world destruction?

WHAT YOU CAN DO NOW

[16] Jehovah God is going to save persons who sincerely want to live under his righteous rule. He will not force any to live in his promised new order under circumstances they themselves say they do not want. But their lack of desire is not going to hold God back from blessing those who do love righteousness. Therefore, those whom he preserves through the coming world destruction will be ones who prove their genuine acceptance of his divine rulership now. They become 'marked' for survival by putting on the "new personality," conforming their lives to God's ways and giving evidence that they truly are dedicated, baptized disciples of God's Son. They actively share in doing the will of God. Thereby they "choose life" and blessings, not death. (Colossians 3:5-10; Deuteronomy 30:15, 16, 19) Will you thus choose life?

[17] Loyalty and submission to God are required, and these things involve worship. Christ Jesus said: "The hour is coming, and it is now, when the true worshipers will worship the Father with spirit and truth, for, indeed, the Father is looking for suchlike ones to worship him." (John 4:23) Survival of the coming world destruction therefore requires our abandoning all false worship and zealously participating in true worship.

[18] Unending blessings await those who take this course that leads to survival. Consider now some of the grand things that God promises for those putting faith in his Word and proving that faith by positive action.

16-18. (a) How does a person become 'marked' for survival through the coming world destruction? (b) So, what action must be taken, first as to false worship, and then as to true worship?

CHAPTER 9

Peace and Security Earth Wide
—A Reliable Hope

THIS earth could be a most pleasant and interesting place in which to live—if truly
peaceful, secure conditions prevailed earth wide.
Though it is far from that now, the Bible foretells that the earth will yet become a splendid
home for mankind, one in which the human family will be able to enjoy life to the full.

2 Just what are the blessings promised, and
how can we be sure that they will be fulfilled?

SOLID BASIS FOR CONFIDENCE

3 There are basic laws that control the universe.
Many of them we take for granted. Sunrise, sun-
set, moon phases and seasons come and go in a
manner that contributes to the stability of human living. Men draw up calendars and plan
activities years ahead, knowing that the move-
ments of the sun, moon and planets are reliable.
What can we learn from this?

4 The Maker of those laws is reliable; what he
says and does is dependable. It is over his name,
as the Creator of heaven and earth, that the
Bible's promises concerning a righteous new order are made. (Isaiah 45:18, 19) In a person's
daily routine of life, it is the normal thing to

1, 2. What conditions, foretold in the Bible, would make this
earth a most pleasant place to live?
3, 4. (a) What do we learn from the reliability of the basic laws
that control the universe? (b) Who is the Maker of those laws,
and so in what else do we have good reason to put our trust?

rely in some measure on other people—on those who bring food to the market to sell, those who deliver the mail, and close friends. Should we not place far, far more confidence in God and in the certainty of the fulfillment of his promises?—Isaiah 55:10, 11.

⁵ It is true that men, for selfish reasons, often prove unreliable. But all of God's promises contained in the Bible are clearly for our good, not to satisfy any selfishness on His part. He does not need anything from us; nor does our believing his Word work to the selfish gain of any men. But God does find delight in those who put faith in him due to their love for him and their appreciation of his ways.—Psalm 50:10-12, 14, 15 [49:10-12, 14, 15, *Dy*].

⁶ Then, too, the Bible appeals to our powers of reason; it does not demand blind faith or credulity. In fact, it defines true faith as "the *assured expectation* of things hoped for, the *evident demonstration of realities* though not beheld." (Hebrews 11:1) In the Bible, God gives us a sound basis for faith. That basis becomes more and more evident as we grow in knowledge of God's Word and see how true it proves to be in our own lives and in the fulfillment of its prophecies.—Psalm 34:8-10 [33:9-11, *Dy*].

⁷ The Bible's promises of future blessings go far beyond what men dare to offer. Yet those promises do not require us to believe things that go against all human experience. Nor are they contrary to what it is normal for a human to

---

5. Is there any selfish motivation in what God has promised so that we have reason to doubt that he will do what he has said?
6. What kind of faith does the Bible help us to acquire?
7. As we examine the Bible's promises of future blessings, what should we not expect belief in them to require of us?

desire. Consider some of these grand blessings and see how this is true.

EARTH TO BECOME A GARDEN HOME

⁸ To many persons the word "paradise" conveys the idea of something unearthly, even unreal. But "paradise" comes from similar words used in ancient times (Hebrew, *par·des'*; Persian, *pai·ri·dae'za;* Greek, *pa·ra'dei·sos*), words that were used to describe things then actually existing on earth. These words all have the basic idea of a 'beautiful park' or 'parklike garden.' As in ancient times, so today there are many such places, some of them parks of great size. And man has a natural yearning for their beauty. The Bible promises that the day will come when this whole planet will be such a parklike garden or paradise.

⁹ When God created the first human pair he gave them as a home the Garden of Eden, which name means Paradise of Pleasure. Paradise was not to be limited to that one location, however. As the Bible relates: "God blessed them and God said to them: 'Be fruitful and become many and fill the earth and subdue it.'" (Genesis 1:28; 2:8, 9) This would involve spreading the boundaries of Paradise to the ends of the earth. The disobedient course of Adam and Eve did not bring to an end that divinely stated purpose. Showing that a Paradise earth was still God's purpose, Christ Jesus promised a man who died alongside him, and who showed faith in Jesus as God's Son, that he would have the opportunity to live

---

8, 9. (a) What idea should be conveyed to our minds by the term "paradise"? (b) Has such a thing ever existed on earth? (c) What shows that it is God's purpose for Paradise to prevail earth wide?

in such earthly Paradise. (Luke 23:39-43) How will this come about?

[10] In the coming "great tribulation" God promises that he will clear away all obstacles to such a paradise by bringing to ruin those ruining the earth. (Revelation 11:18) God will thus do what human governments never could do. He will clear out all those who selfishly pollute and ravage the earth to satisfy commercial greed, all who wage devastating wars due to thirst for power, all who misuse the earth because they lack gratitude and respect for the bountiful gifts that God has provided.

[11] The whole earth will then blossom forth with beauty; freshness and cleanness will then come to its air, water and land. This restoration of Paradise is not something beyond believing or contrary to human experience. Many centuries ago, when the nation of Israel came out of captivity in Babylon, Jehovah God restored them to their homeland. When they returned, the land was a desolate waste. Yet, because of God's blessing on them and their work, the land soon changed so that neighboring peoples exclaimed: 'It has become like the garden of Eden!' Where thickets of thorns and stinging nettles had grown, now juniper and myrtle trees flourished. The land became bountifully productive, removing any threat of hunger and famine. (Ezekiel 36:29, 30, 35; Isaiah 35:1, 2; 55:13) What God did then in that small area of Palestine he promises to do on a global scale, so that all persons living will enjoy

---

10. At Revelation 11:18, what obstacles to Paradise does God promise to remove?
11. (a) What historical event shows that restoration of the earth to a paradise state is not contrary to human experience? (b) In what promised blessing does this strengthen our faith?

the divinely provided pleasures of life in Paradise.—Psalm 67:6, 7 [66:7, 8, *Dy*]; Isaiah 25:6.

END OF POVERTY AND ECONOMIC SLAVERY

[12] It is well known that poverty and bondage to the economic system are found earth wide. There could be no real enjoyment of life in God's new order if this condition were not remedied, if millions went on doing labor that provided just the bare means of living, or doing work that is monotonous and makes a man an impersonal cog in a huge machine.

[13] God's will for man in this regard is seen in the way he directed matters with ancient Israel. There, each family received a hereditary possession of land. (Judges 2:6) Even though this could be sold and even though individuals also could sell themselves into servitude if they fell into debt, Jehovah still made provisions to guard against the building up of huge landholdings or any long-term enslavement of people. How?

[14] By means of the provisions in the Law he gave his people. The seventh year of servitude was a 'year of release' when any Israelite thus in bondage must be set free. Also, every fiftieth year was a "Jubilee" year for the whole nation, a year in which to "proclaim liberty in the land to all its inhabitants." (Deuteronomy 15:1-9; Leviticus 25:10) Then any hereditary possession sold was returned to its original owner, and all in servitude were released, even though seven years had not elapsed. It was a joyful time of

---

12. What economic and working conditions must be remedied if we are to have real enjoyment in life?
13-15. (a) Where do we find a historical example that shows us what God's will for man is in this regard? (b) How did that arrangement contribute to the security and enjoyment of life of each individual and family?

happy family reunion and a 'new start' in life economically. Thus, no land could be sold for all time, but its sale was, in effect, just a 'lease' that would end, at the latest, in the Jubilee year. —Leviticus 25:8-24.

¹⁵ All this contributed splendidly to the economic stability of the nation and the security and peace of each family. When observed, it kept the nation from falling into the sad picture we see today in so many lands where only two classes exist, the extremely rich and the extremely poor. The benefits to the individual strengthened the nation, for none needed to be underprivileged and crushed by bad economic conditions. As reported during the reign of King Solomon, who looked to Jehovah for wisdom: "Judah and Israel continued to dwell in security, everyone under his own vine and under his own fig tree." (1 Kings 4:25 [3 Kings 4:25, *Dy*]) Today many persons cannot really employ their talents and initiative, because they are trapped in an economic system that locks them in, making them serve the desires of one person or a small group of persons. Under God's law the industrious person was aided to contribute his full abilities to the welfare and enjoyment of all. This gives us at least a small-scale idea of the measure of personal freedom and the sense of personal worth and dignity that those gaining life in God's new order will enjoy.

¹⁶ Earth wide the prophecy of Micah 4:3, 4 will see major fulfillment. Peace-loving persons living under God's righteous rule will "sit, each one under his vine and under his fig tree, and there will be no one making them tremble; for

16. As to living conditions and one's economic situation, what will God's kingdom provide for all of us who are its subjects?

the very mouth of Jehovah of armies has spoken it." None of the subjects of God's kingdom will live in squalid slums or crowded tenements. They will have land and homes that are their own. (Isaiah 65:21, 22) The king, Christ Jesus, long ago promised that the 'mild-tempered ones will inherit the earth,' and he has 'all authority in heaven and earth' to see that this is the case. —Matthew 5:5; 28:18.

ENDURING HEALTH AND LIFE

[17] None of these conditions, however, could make your life genuinely peaceful and secure as long as sickness, old age and death clouded the future. Is it unreasonable or contrary to human experience to hope for relief from these things? It certainly is not contrary to man's nature to *want* this, for men have spent lifetimes and untold sums of money searching for the means to accomplish it.

[18] Rather than the hope of enduring health and life being unreasonable, is it not the opposite that is unreasonable—that, just when humans reach an age where they begin to have a fine fund of knowledge, experience and ability to do worthwhile things, they then die? On the other hand, there are trees that live for thousands of years. Why should man, who is endowed with intelligence, live for only a fraction of the time that some unconscious, unintelligent vegetation does? Should he not reasonably live far, far longer?

[19] The book *Science Year* of 1967 states that

17-19. (a) What shows that good health and long life are natural desires of mankind? (b) What facts about human life and about vegetation make man's short life-span seem strange? (c) What is there about the human brain that shows it is very reasonable to believe that man was designed to live forever?

for specialists in the study of aging "the aging process is still largely a mystery."[32] Mystifying to scientists, too, is the fact that the human brain is obviously designed to take in virtually unlimited amounts of information. As biochemist Isaac Asimov points out, the brain's "filing system" is "perfectly capable of handling any load of learning and memory which the human being is likely to put upon it—and a billion times more than that quantity, too."[33] That means that your brain is capable of handling not only any load you might put on it in a lifetime of seventy or eighty years, but *a thousand million times more!* No wonder man has such a thirst for knowledge, such desire to learn to do and accomplish things. Yet he is blocked by his shortness of life. Is it reasonable that man should have such a fantastic organ as the human brain is and then never get to use more than a tiny fraction of its potential? Is it not far more reasonable that, as the Bible shows, Jehovah God designed man to live forever on earth and gave him a brain admirably suited to that purpose?

[20] The Bible shows that originally man had the opportunity of living forever, but lost it through rebellion; that "through one man [Adam] sin entered into the world and death through sin, and thus death spread to all men because they had all sinned." (Romans 5:12) Human experience agrees, for sin and death are universal among mankind. But the Bible also contains God's promise that, in the restored Paradise, "death will be no more, neither will mourning nor outcry nor pain be anymore." (Revelation

---

20. Just what does the Bible say that God has promised to do for mankind in regard to the effects of sin, including death itself?

21:3, 4; 7:16, 17) It clearly states that everlasting life, free from the effects of sin, is God's purpose for mankind. (Romans 5:21; 6:23) More than this, it promises that the blessings of God's new order will be opened up for the many millions who have died in the past. How? By a resurrection from death, yes, by the emptying of the common grave of all mankind. Concerning this, Jesus Christ confidently foretold: "The hour is coming in which all those in the memorial tombs will hear his voice and come out."—John 5:28, 29.

[21] Modern medical scientists today produce "miracle drugs" and perform surgical feats that would have seemed incredible centuries ago. Should we doubt that man's Creator can do far grander and more astounding things to restore righteous-hearted persons to vibrant health, even reverse the aging process—all without resorting to hospitals, operating rooms and artificial organs? In his considerateness, God has provided us with the evidence that such blessings are not too much to hope for.

[22] He empowered his Son while on earth to perform powerful works of healing. These works assure us that no weakness, defect or disease is beyond God's power to heal. When a man whose flesh was filled with leprosy implored Jesus to heal him, Jesus compassionately touched the man and said: "Be made clean." And, as the historical record says, "immediately his leprosy was cleansed away." (Matthew 8:2, 3) Jesus did not do these things in some isolated place, out of public view. The historian Matthew Levi reports: "Great crowds approached him, having along

---

21, 22. Why is the prospect of restoration to full health not something that is too much to hope for?

with them people that were lame, maimed, blind, dumb, and many otherwise, and they fairly threw them at his feet, and he cured them; so that the crowd felt amazement . . . and they glorified the God of Israel." (Matthew 15:30, 31) Read for yourself the account at John 9:1-21 as an example of how factual and true to life the historical report of such cures is. These events are testified to by many witnesses, including a doctor, the physician Luke.—Mark 7:32-37; Luke 5:12-14, 17-25; 6:6-11; Colossians 4:14.

²³ For similar reasons we need not view as beyond belief the clear Bible promise that "there is going to be a resurrection" of the dead. (Acts 24:15) Humans today can record a person's voice, appearance and actions on a small piece of film or videotape, so that even years after his death these can be reproduced. Should not the One who created man, who logically knows the precise atomic and molecular structure of man, be able to do far more? If man-made computers can store up and coordinate literally billions of pieces of data, should not God be able to remember precisely the personalities of individuals so as to restore these to life?—Job 14:13.

²⁴ Again, Jehovah God has kindly given us the means for strengthening our faith in such a tremendous hope. He granted his Son power to demonstrate on a small scale what he will do on a massive scale during his righteous rule over earth. Christ Jesus resurrected dead persons, often doing so in full view of onlookers. The man Lazarus, whom he resurrected near Jerusalem, had even been dead long enough for his body

<hr>

23, 24. Why is it not unreasonable to believe that the dead actually can and will be restored to life under God's kingdom?

to begin to decompose. Thus the resurrection hope is seen to have a solid basis.—Luke 7:11-17; 8:40-42, 49-56; John 11:38-44.

THE EARTH'S ABILITY TO CONTAIN SUCH POPULATION

[25] Can this planet provide comfortable living space for such a population as would result from the resurrection of the dead? In 1960, Dr. Albert L. Elder, as president of the American Chemical Society, stated:

> "It took over 5000 years of human history up to about 1820 to reach a world population of 1.1 billion. Within the following century, population doubled. Now, it stands at about 2.8 billion and could reach 3 billion early in the 1960's [as it did]. Thus, in less than 50 *years* there has been an increase in population equivalent to that which occurred during the first 50 *centuries*."[34]

[26] Those alive today, therefore, represent a sizable portion of the total that has ever lived on earth. In fact, in 1966 it was stated: "It is now estimated that 25 per cent of all the people who have ever lived are alive today."[35] On this basis the total population throughout all human history could be estimated at some 14,000,000,000 persons. The earth's land area is more than 36,000,000,000 acres. That would allow more than two and a half acres per person. Not only would this provide space for food production, but also it would allow for forests, mountains and so forth with no undue crowding in the paradise earth. Then, too, it must be remembered that the Bible shows that by no means all those now living will survive and live in that new order.

25, 26. When the dead are resurrected, where will there be room for everyone to live?

²⁷ But could the earth produce enough food for so many people? Scientists today claim that it could do so even under present-day conditions. *Time* magazine (July 13, 1970) reported that the United Nations Food and Agriculture Organization "now maintains that the world's agricultural potential is great enough to feed 157 billion people." That is far, far more than the total number estimated of those who have ever lived on earth.

²⁸ We should note that God's purpose originally stated to the first human pair was that they should "fill the earth and subdue it," extending Eden's limits to the farthest reaches of earth. (Genesis 1:28) This would mean, not overrunning the earth with people, but filling it to a comfortable extent, to an extent that would still permit the 'subdued' earth to be a global park like man's original parklike home. So, this divine command indicates that, in God's due time and way, reproduction would eventually cease among mankind. To God, who endowed man with reproductive abilities, that presents no big problem.

A SURE FOUNDATION FOR ENDURING HAPPINESS

²⁹ Even though you could live in beautiful surroundings, have material prosperity, do interesting work and enjoy relatively good health, this would still not guarantee your lasting happiness. There are persons today who have these things and yet

---

27. Could the earth produce enough food for all those people?
28. Why is there no danger that, with people living forever, the earth would in time become overcrowded?
29, 30. (a) What effect do relationships with other people have on a person's happiness? (b) How do we know that those who gain eternal life in God's new order will be only persons who truly contribute to the peace and security of their fellowmen?

are unhappy. Why? Because of their relationships with the people around them, people who may be selfish, quarrelsome, hypocritical or hateful. Enduring happiness in God's new order will come in large measure from the changed attitude of people, all over the earth. Their love and respect for God and their seeking to carry out his purposes will bring *spiritual* prosperity. Without that, material prosperity becomes vain, unsatisfying and empty.

[30] Even more than having material things, pleasure comes from being around people who are kind, humble, friendly, people you can really love and trust, and who feel that way about you. (Psalm 133:1 [132:1, *Dy*]; Proverbs 15:17) Love of God is what ensures true love of neighbor, which will make life so pleasant in His righteous new order. Those whom God will favor with eternal life will all be persons who have proved their love for him and for their fellowman. With such persons for your neighbors, friends and work companions, you will be able to enjoy real peace and security and enduring happiness. —1 John 4:7, 8, 20, 21.

[31] Inasmuch as such a grand prospect is open to you, the course of practical wisdom is to find out what is required to lay hold of it. Now is the time to bring your life into harmony with the righteous requirements that God has set out in his Word for those who will be spared through the coming "great tribulation."—2 Peter 3:11-13.

---

31. If we really want life in God's new order, what should we do now?

CHAPTER 10

Are You Willing to Face the Truth in Your Life?

TRUTH is very desirable. If acted upon, it can protect you from harm or loss and thus contribute to your happiness, security and welfare. This is especially the case respecting the truth about what is ahead for this generation.

[2] In the light of the facts presented earlier in this book, you may well agree that man cannot bring true peace and security. You may realize that what the Bible says is the truth—that only God can solve the problems facing mankind, and that he will do so by means of the kingdom that he has entrusted to his Son. If so, would it not be wisdom on your part to act in harmony with what you now know to be the truth? (James 1:22) What does this involve?

[3] The Bible sets out standards to be met by those whom God will preserve into his righteous new order. These standards require changes in the life of everyone who wants to become a servant of God. It is true that not everyone has lived a life that, from a human standpoint, is considered to be bad. Nevertheless, the changes one must make are of no little consequence; they involve a completely new outlook on life. That is why Romans 12:2 says: "Quit being fashioned

---

1, 2. (a) How can truth benefit us? (b) What do you personally believe to be the real source from which true peace and security will come?
3. How important are the changes that a person must make in his life if he wants to be preserved by God into His new order?

after this system of things, but be transformed by making your mind over, that you may prove to yourselves the good and acceptable and perfect will of God."

[4] Such a transformation will affect the basis on which we determine what is right and what is wrong. In the past we may have relied on the imperfect opinions of fellowmen or tried to set our own standards of conduct. But now we realize that it was by setting their own standard as to good and bad that Adam and Eve rejected God as their Ruler, with disastrous consequences. If we want God's approval, we must look to him for direction, determining what is right and what is wrong on the basis of what is in the Bible. In choosing to submit to God's will, we are in no danger of being misled. As Psalm 119:151 [118:151, *Dy*] says, 'All his commandments are truth,' and, therefore, conforming to them means 'walking in the way of truth.' (Psalm 86:11 [85:11, *Dy*]) Is that not really what you want to do?

THE NEED FOR COUNSEL AND DISCIPLINE

[5] If a person is going to make changes in his life, he must be willing to acknowledge wrong and see the need for making improvement. Do we not all make mistakes and therefore need correction? "There is no man that does not sin," says the Bible. (1 Kings 8:46 [3 Kings 8:46, *Dy*]) Yet many people are unwilling to admit mistakes. Why? Pride stands in their way. Instead of humbly acknowledging their wrong, they often blame others. This only worsens the problem.

---

4. If we are really going to 'walk in the way of the truth,' on what basis must we determine what is right and what is wrong?
5. (a) If we are going to make changes in our lives, what truth about ourselves must we be willing to face? (b) What often prevents a person from admitting a mistake, and with what results?

⁶ Equally great a problem is that, being imperfect, we do not always discern the proper course to take. We can even be deceived into thinking that a harmful course is quite all right. (Proverbs 16:25) So we need counsel and discipline from a source higher than man in order to act wisely, in a way that will be in our best interests and in the best interests of fellow humans. The Source of this discipline is Jehovah God. Therefore Proverbs 3:11 counsels: "The discipline of Jehovah, O my son, do not reject."

⁷ How does Jehovah provide this discipline? He does this by means of his Word, the Holy Bible. So when we read the Bible or have what it says drawn to our attention by a fellow believer and come to appreciate that we are in some way not measuring up to divine requirements, we are receiving God's discipline. By accepting that discipline as right and applying it, we prove that we are facing up to the truth. We acknowledge God's right to give us direction and show that we are the kind of people he desires in his new order. Our life depends upon heeding divine discipline.—Proverbs 4:13.

⁸ Surely if we are going to benefit from God's discipline, we must be honest with ourselves. It would do us little good to put on a pretense when observed by others, only to go back to our former ways when out of their view. For us to play the role of hypocrites would not help us to change

6. To what source should we look for counsel and discipline, and why?
7. (a) How does the discipline from Jehovah reach us? (b) Our accepting and applying such discipline shows what about us?
8. (a) Why would we actually be hurting ourselves if we put on a pretense of accepting discipline but did not really change our ways? (b) Why is it comforting to know that Jehovah sees us wherever we are?

from our wrong ways; it would only dull our consciences. Then, too, though men may look upon us with admiration, we cannot deceive the Creator. What we do does not escape his notice. Proverbs 15:3 tells us: "The eyes of Jehovah are in every place, keeping watch upon the bad ones and the good ones." Knowing that Jehovah God is watching should hold us back from doing wrong. At the same time we can find comfort in the assurance that he looks favorably 'upon the good ones' and will support them in time of trial. Who are "the good ones" whom God thus favors?

"SPEAK TRUTHFULLY WITH ONE ANOTHER"

[9] Though not claiming to adhere strictly to God's Word, most people today do not consider themselves to be dishonest. But how many are there who consistently speak the truth? Instead, is it not the case that many persons are willing to conceal truth or speak only what they believe will further their own ends? While this is viewed as normal in the world, this does not make it right, does it? The world of mankind alienated from God "is lying in the power of the wicked one." That "wicked one," Satan the Devil, is "the father of the lie." Lying originated with him. (1 John 5:19; John 8:44) So it should not surprise a person if he finds that he needs to make quite a change in his view as to truthfulness if he is going to "quit being fashioned after this system of things."

[10] There is good reason for wanting to be honest.

---

9. (a) When it comes to speaking the truth, what is accepted as normal in the world? Why? (b) So, if a person is going to "quit being fashioned after this system of things," what change is required?
10. How does the vicious cycle of dishonesty work against true peace and security?

Nothing undermines peace and security more than a failure to be honest at all times and everywhere—at home, in work or business, in recreation and social relations. When people do not keep their word, when they break promises, deceive or cheat, no one gains. The victims of dishonesty are disappointed and often become bitter and angry. Aside from emotional and mental pressures, dishonesty is also responsible for physical injury and even death. This has been the case when, for example, poor workmanship, inferior materials and deceptive claims contributed to serious accidents. The person who thinks he is gaining through his dishonesty is at the same time losing through the dishonesty of others. He, too, pays higher prices for goods and services because both employees and customers steal. Dishonesty thus brings about a vicious cycle. As more people take advantage of others, frustrations, disappointments, violence, injuries and deaths multiply.

[11] In view of such bad fruitage, Jehovah God could never approve of dishonesty and lying. Among the things that "Jehovah does hate" are lying, perjury, false weights and false scales. (Proverbs 6:16-19; 20:23) Habitual liars will not have any share in the blessings that God has in store for those loving him. (Revelation 21:8) Is this not what we would expect from a righteous God? If God were to continue tolerating those desiring to profit by deceit at their neighbor's expense, how could anyone feel secure in His new order?

[12] The Bible is therefore not speaking lightly

11. How does Jehovah feel about dishonesty and lying?
12, 13. (a) What does the Bible itself say about truthful speech? (b) What bearing does our honesty have on whether we can serve Jehovah as his witnesses?

when it commands: "Speak truthfully with one another." (Zechariah 8:16; Ephesians 4:25) As to promises or agreements, our "Yes" should mean *Yes,* and our "No," *No.* (James 5:12) It should not take an oath to make our speech more dependable or believable. If we want to represent "Jehovah the God of truth," we must be consistent about speaking truth. (Psalm 31:5 [30:6, *Dy*]) If a person does not tell the truth, he cannot gain the respect of God or of his fellowmen, nor can he represent God as one of His witnesses. Said the psalmist: "To the wicked one God will have to say: 'What right do you have to enumerate my regulations, and that you may bear my covenant in your mouth? Your mouth you have let loose to what is bad, and your tongue you keep attached to deception.' "—Psalm 50:16, 19 [49:16, 19, *Dy*].

¹³ But some may wonder, Can a person carry on in this world and be truthful and honest? Can he make a go of it in business without doing what everybody else is doing?

GOD CARES FOR THOSE APPLYING THE TRUTH

¹⁴ To say that a person cannot make a living without being dishonest would be to say that God does not care about those who love him. This is not true. It is contrary to the experience of God's servants for thousands of years. (Hebrews 13:5, 6) The psalmist David, for example, observed: "A young man I used to be, I have also grown old, and yet I have not seen anyone righteous left entirely, nor his offspring looking for bread." (Psalm 37:25 [36:25, *Dy*]) This does not mean that righteous persons do not experience diffi-

---

14. How does the Bible help us to appreciate that it is possible to make a living in this world without being dishonest?

culties or hard times. David himself had been forced to live for a time as an outcast from society, but he had the necessities of life.

[15] The appeal on the part of true worship is not one of materialistic gain; however, Jesus Christ did teach his followers that it is proper to pray to God to bless their efforts to obtain the "bread for the day according to the day's requirement." (Luke 11:2, 3) Not minimizing their need for food and covering, he assured his disciples: "Your heavenly Father knows you need all these things." But he urged them: "Keep on, then, seeking first the kingdom and his righteousness, and all these other things will be added to you." (Matthew 6:25-34) Do you believe that? If so, you will not be tempted to discard God's righteous standards just because other people do. Instead, you will appreciate the wisdom of what is recorded at 1 Timothy 6:6-8, which says: "To be sure, it is a means of great gain, this godly devotion along with self-sufficiency. For we have brought nothing into the world, and neither can we carry anything out. So, having sustenance and covering, we shall be content with these things."

[16] Following this admonition requires a viewpoint that is quite different from what is common in the world today. This, then, is also involved in 'making our minds over.' Contentment with life's necessities prevents us from making money our god and allowing ourselves to be enslaved in its service. (Matthew 6:24) It safeguards one against making material things the main objective in life and being tempted to cheat and to take ad-

---

15. What did Jesus say about God's interest in our obtaining material things to sustain life?
16. How can our applying the truth expressed in those scriptures safeguard us?

vantage of other persons to get these. (Proverbs 28:20; 1 Timothy 6:9, 10) Those who make riches their goal may think that it represents security and happiness. But is that the case? Is it not rather true, as the Bible says, that a "lover of silver will not be satisfied with silver, neither any lover of wealth with income"? (Ecclesiastes 5:10) Those who have much want more. Often they sacrifice their health and the enjoyment of being with their family to obtain it. Rather than feeling secure, they live in fear of losing what they have.

[17] When a person gives in to the desire for wealth, he is not facing up to the fact that, as Jesus Christ said, "even when a person has an abundance his life does not result from the things he possesses." (Luke 12:15) Far better it is to put faith in God's ability to provide for his servants. In over two hundred lands among the more than one and a half million witnesses of Jehovah there is living proof that God does provide. Under all forms of government and in every kind of legitimate employment, Witnesses of all races and backgrounds are able to continue to live happy lives, with their needs supplied. True, they experience ridicule and, in some places, physical persecution because of their faith. Nevertheless, their faith in God's ability to provide even when honesty puts them at a seeming disadvantage has been rewarded. They have gained the respect of fellowmen and are often preferred as employees because of their honesty. Even in

---

17. (a) When a person sets his heart on the acquiring of material wealth, what truth is he ignoring? (b) What evidence is there that it is practical in our day to apply the principles of honesty and truthfulness in making a living?

this dishonest world, people still want to deal with those who are trustworthy. But, more important, the upright ones enjoy a clean conscience because of their honesty; and, because they do the will of God, they have the prospect of eternal life in his new order.

[18] In the past, before becoming Jehovah's Christian witnesses, they followed the ways of the world to a greater or lesser degree. But after studying the Bible and coming to a knowledge of the truth, they dropped bad practices. Now they are striving hard to continue making improvement. They are endeavoring to exhibit "good fidelity to the full, so that they may adorn the teaching of our Savior, God, in all things." (Titus 2:10) It has not always been easy for them to face up to the truth and make changes in their life. But love for truth has helped them to act in harmony with it.

[19] Do you have similar love for truth? If you do, you are the kind of person God is looking for to preserve alive into his new order. Those whom he accepts "must worship with spirit and *truth*." (John 4:24) This marks them as different from the world around them. There are also other ways in which they must differ from the world if they truly are to be well pleasing to Jehovah. What are these?

18, 19. (a) Why have these people changed their lives to conform to these standards? (b) What kind of persons is God looking for to preserve into his new order?

CHAPTER 11

Survivors Must Be "No Part of the World"

WE HUMANS are all "in the world," that is, living among the world of mankind. Yet, Jesus Christ said that his followers must be "no part of the world." (John 17:11, 14) What did he mean? If we hope to be among those surviving to life in God's new order, we need to understand this.

² First consider what being "no part of the world" does *not* mean. It does not mean that we isolate ourselves from people. It does not mean living like hermits in a cave or withdrawing into a monastery or other remote place. To the contrary, the night before his death Jesus prayed to his Father on behalf of his disciples, saying: "I request you, *not to take them out of the world,* but to watch over them because of the wicked one. They are no part of the world, just as I am no part of the world."—John 17:15, 16.

³ Rather than hide themselves from people, Jesus' disciples were 'sent forth into the world,' to make known the truth. (John 17:18) They were to serve as "the light of the world," letting the light of truth shine before men so that these might see how God's truth affects people's lives for good.—Matthew 5:14-16.

1, 2. (a) What did Jesus say about the relationship of his disciples to the world? (b) What does that *not* mean, and why?
3, 4. (a) In what activities is it necessary for Christians to have contact with people of the world? (b) But what must they avoid?

⁴ Christians, of necessity, have contact with many people as they work to support themselves and their families and as they declare the good news of God's kingdom to mankind. So, as the apostle Paul shows, they are not expected to "get out of the world" in a physical way. They cannot entirely "quit mixing in company" with people of the world. But they can and must keep the wrong ways that the majority of mankind practice from infecting them and the Christian congregation.—1 Corinthians 5:9-11.

⁵ So, they must be like Noah and his family. In Noah's day "all men had lived corrupt lives on earth." (Genesis 6:12, *NE*) But Noah and his family were different. By refusing to join the rest of mankind in their ungodly course and by preaching righteousness, Noah "condemned the world," showed it to be inexcusably out of harmony with God's will. (Hebrews 11:7; 2 Peter 2:5) That is why, when the global flood brought an end to ungodly mankind, he and his family survived. They were "in the world" but at the same time were "no part of the world."—Genesis 6:9-13; 7:1; Matthew 24:38, 39.

WHAT IS PROPER LOVE FOR PEOPLE OF THE WORLD?

⁶ Would your becoming "no part of the world" mean that you become a 'hater of mankind'? Not at all. Instead, you should imitate Jehovah God. As recorded at John 3:16, Jesus Christ tells us: "God loved the world [of mankind] so much that he gave his only-begotten Son, in order that everyone exercising faith in him might not be

---

5. How is the needed separateness from the world illustrated in the case of Noah and his family?
6. Is it proper to show any love toward people of the world?

destroyed but have everlasting life." God's kindness and compassion toward people of all sorts sets the example for us to follow.—Matthew 5:44-48.

⁷ But does not the apostle John tell us, "Do not be loving either the world or the things in the world. If anyone loves the world, the love of the Father is not in him"? If God loved the world, why did the apostle say this?—1 John 2:15.

⁸ The Bible shows that God loved the world of mankind simply as *humans,* people in an imperfect, dying state who were in desperate need of help, whether they appreciated it or not. But he did not love the *ungodly qualities* they had and that manifested themselves in wrong desires. And he did not love the *ungodly deeds* they committed. The apostle John warned against loving the wrong desires and deeds of the world of mankind, stating: "Because everything in the world—the desire of the flesh and the desire of the eyes and the showy display of one's means of life—does not originate with the Father, but originates with the world. Furthermore, the world is passing away and so is its desire, but he that does the will of God remains forever."—1 John 2:15-17.

⁹ Yes, those desires of the flesh and of the eyes and the desire for personal exaltation did 'originate with the world'—they were what developed in mankind's first parents and led them into a course of rebellion. (Genesis 3:1-6, 17) Wrong desire caused them to seek independence from God so that they could follow selfish interests out of harmony with his will. Following

7, 8. (a) What did the apostle John say about loving the world? (b) What does that mean, and how do John's further comments show this?
9, 10. (a) How can it be said that these desires 'originate with the world'? (b) What effect have these desires had on mankind?

these selfish desires led to breaking God's laws.

[10] Consider what you see around you in our time. Do not most of the people today build their lives around the desires of the flesh and of the eyes and the "showy display of one's means of life"? Is it not these things that shape the hopes and interests of the great mass of mankind, governing the way they act and their dealings with one another? Yes, and this has led to their breaking of God's laws. Because of this the history of mankind is one long record of disunity and war, of immorality and crime, of commercial greed and oppression, of proud ambition and striving for fame and power.

[11] We can see, then, the difference between loving the world as God did and loving its wrong desires and practices, which the apostle condemns. God's love for the world of mankind was expressed for the very purpose of opening the way for them to become free from those sinful desires and their bad results, including death itself. He expressed that love at great cost to himself, giving his own Son as a sacrifice to ransom mankind. But for anyone who rejects that sacrifice and willfully continues in disobedience, the Bible says that "the wrath of God remains upon him." —John 3:16, 36; Romans 5:6-8.

[12] What, then, about us? Do we love persons of the world because of sincere concern for them as fellow *humans,* people who need help in order to find the way to life in God's favor? Or do we love the very things that hold them back from becoming God's servants—the independent way

---

11. So, then, why is God's love for the world not inconsistent with what the apostle John condemns?
12. How can we analyze whether the love we may have for persons of the world is pleasing to God or not?

in which they go about breaking God's laws to satisfy their selfish fleshly interests and their concern for their own importance and glory rather than that of God? If we are attracted to people and love to be with them for these bad qualities, then we are loving the world in the way the apostle warned against.

[13] Because many persons in Jesus' day loved the world's bad ways, they avoided taking a bold stand as Jesus' disciples. They did not want to lose their popularity and position among the people in their social and religious circles. They loved the praise of men rather than the approval of God. (John 12:42, 43) Some performed works of charity and did other religious acts—but primarily because they wanted to be looked up to by men, yes, by the world of mankind. (Matthew 6:1-6; 23:5-7; Mark 12:38-40) Do you not see people, even large numbers of those in Christendom, showing this same love of the world's wrong course today? Yet the Bible shows this is not the course leading to survival.

KEEPING FREE FROM CONTROL BY "THE RULER OF THIS WORLD"

[14] God's own Son was subjected to temptation along these same lines. The effort was made to stir up in him selfish desire of the flesh and the eyes and to get him to make a showy display to impress people—to become like the world. He was even offered rulership over all the kingdoms of the world with their glory. He flatly rejected that appeal. He knew how to show love for the

13. How could love for the world hold a person back from serving God?
14. Who subjected Jesus to temptation when he was on earth, and with what outcome?

world in harmony with his Father's will. But from whom did that appeal to selfishness come? From the one who first challenged Jehovah God's sovereignty, the same one who induced our first parents to prove false to their Creator, namely, Satan the Devil. (Luke 4:5-8) This is a vital point for us to recognize. Why?

¹⁵ Because it shows that the world of mankind in general, including its worldly kingdoms and other rulerships, has God's adversary as its invisible ruler. Jesus himself spoke of that chief opposer of God as "the ruler of this world." (John 12:31; 14:30; 2 Corinthians 4:4) The apostle Paul also referred to "wicked spirit forces" or demons under Satan's control as constituting invisible 'governments, authorities and world rulers of this darkness,' against whom Christians need defense through spiritual armor.—Ephesians 6:10-13.

¹⁶ Only a minority has ever stayed free from the control of this invisible ruler and his forces. But the "world," that is, the mass of mankind in general, "is lying in the power of the wicked one." By demonistic influence he 'misleads the entire inhabited earth,' including the earthly rulers, steering them onto a collision course against God and his kingdom by Christ Jesus.—1 John 5:19; Revelation 12:9; 16:13, 14; 19:11-18.

¹⁷ Does this sound hard to believe? Yet, do not most people of this world clearly manifest the "spirit"—the dominant attitude and impelling force—and the works that characterize God's adversary? World wide we see the lying, decep-

15. Show from your Bible who "the ruler of this world" is.
16. How much of the world has been misled by Satan and is in his power?
17. (a) What does the "spirit" manifested by the world testify as to the one who is leading mankind? (b) Would it be pleasing to the Creator if we manifested such a spirit?

tion, hatred, violence and murder that the Bible says identifies persons as 'originating with the Devil,' that is, as having him for their spiritual "father." (Ephesians 2:2, 3; John 8:44; 1 John 3:8-12) Surely this spirit of the world does not come from a loving Creator.

[18] Do we not also see the vast majority of the people trusting in human schemes and projects to bring them peace and security on earth? How many persons do you know who really look to God and to his Son's kingdom to solve earth's problems, rather than to human political systems? Yet Jesus said: "My kingdom is no part of this world." His kingdom does not have its "source" in this world, because men do not give it its authority nor set it up nor keep it in power. It is God's own provision. (John 18:36; Isaiah 9:6, 7) So, to be among those hoping to survive when that kingdom comes against all its opponents, we need to recognize the hard fact of Satan's dominance of this world and its systems. We need to maintain freedom therefrom by our firm stand for Jehovah's righteous government by Christ Jesus. —Matthew 6:10, 24, 31-33.

[19] History shows how early Christians, though respectful, law-abiding citizens, were determined to be "no part of the world," even though this brought upon them severe persecution. We read statements such as these:

"Early Christianity was little understood and was regarded with little favor by those who ruled the pagan world. . . . Christians refused to share certain duties of Roman citizens. . . . They would not hold

---

18. How does our attitude concerning rulership show whether we are free from the control of the "ruler of this world"?
19. As testified to by history, in what ways did the early Christians show that they were "no part of the world"?

political office."—*On the Road to Civilization, A World History*, by Heckel and Sigman, pp. 237, 238.

"They refused to take any active part in the civil administration or the military defence of the empire. . . . it was impossible that the Christians, without renouncing a more sacred duty, could assume the character of soldiers, of magistrates, or of princes." —*History of Christianity*, Edward Gibbon, pp. 162, 163.

"Origen [who lived in the second and third centuries of the Common Era] . . . remarks that 'the Christian Church cannot engage in war against any nation. They have learned from their Leader that they are children of peace.' In that period many Christians were martyred for refusing military service. On March 12, 295, Maximilian, the son of a famous Roman veteran, was called upon to serve in the Roman army and he refused, saying simply: 'I am a Christian.' "—H. Ingli James, quoted in *Treasury of the Christian World*, edited by A. Gordon Nasby, p. 369.

[20] By maintaining this freedom from involvement in the world's affairs, Jehovah's servants do not contribute to its strife, its divisive nationalism or racialism, its social conflicts. Their God-directed attitude contributes toward peace and security among men of all sorts. (Acts 10:34, 35) Survivors of the coming "great tribulation" will, in fact, come "out of all nations and tribes and peoples and tongues."—Revelation 7:9, 14.

FRIENDS OF THE WORLD OR FRIENDS OF GOD?

[21] Jesus told his disciples: "If you were part of the world, the world would be fond of what is its own. Now because you are no part of the world,

---

20. To keep free from control by the "ruler of this world," from what divisive activities of the world do Jehovah's servants abstain?
21. Why cannot a person who follows the Bible also expect to be loved by the world?

but I have chosen you out of the world, on this account the world hates you. . . . If they have persecuted me, they will persecute you also." (John 15:19, 20) The simple truth is that the only way to have the world's friendship is to become like it, share its desires, ambitions, prejudices, admire its thinking and philosophies, take up its practices and ways. But supporters of this world resent having their errors exposed or being warned of the dangers to which their course is leading. That is why, if one follows the Bible, upholds its teachings in conduct and manner of life and speaks in favor of it, he simply cannot escape the world's hatred.—John 17:14; 2 Timothy 3:12.

²² So, the Bible shows we have a clear choice. At James 4:4 we read: "Do you not know that the friendship with the world is enmity with God? Whoever, therefore, wants to be a friend of the world is constituting himself an enemy of God." God also has his standards for friendship and they are not in harmony with those of the world of sinful mankind.—Psalm 15:1-5 [14:1-5, Dy].

²³ Our having God's friendship, which leads to survival into his new order, depends upon much more than our belonging or not belonging to certain of this world's organizations. If we manifest the world's *spirit,* share its worldly *viewpoint* of life, then we identify ourselves as friends of the world, not of God. The world's spirit produces the "works of the flesh," things such as "fornication, uncleanness, loose conduct, idolatry, practice of spiritism, enmities, strife, jealousy, fits of anger,

_____

22. What choice as to friendship confronts each one of us?
23. (a) What would show that a person is a friend of the world?
(b) How can we show that we are friends of God?

contentions, divisions, sects, envies, drunken bouts, revelries, and things like these." The Bible clearly says that "those who practice such things will not inherit God's kingdom." Exactly to the contrary, if we are God's friends we will have his spirit with its fruits of "love, joy, peace, long-suffering, kindness, goodness, faith, mildness, self-control." —Galatians 5:19-23.

[24] Whose spirit, then, do *we* reflect? That will help us to determine whose friends we really are. Living as we do in this present evil world, subjected to its influences, we should not be surprised if we find the need to make changes in our lives in order to please God. Worldly people, for example, heap honor and glory on persons whose ambitious drive leads them to great wealth, power or fame. People pattern themselves after such worldly heroes and idols, imitating them in speech, conduct, appearance and dress. Do you want to be identified as an admirer of such people? Their achievements are just the opposite of what God's Word urges us to make our goal in life. The Bible directs us to spiritual wealth and strength and the honor of serving as God's representatives and spokesmen on earth. (1 Timothy 6:17-19; 2 Timothy 1:7, 8; Jeremiah 9:23, 24) The world's commercial propaganda turns people to materialism. They come to believe that their happiness is all wrapped up in material possessions and they give these far greater importance than God's Word or things of spiritual value. Such things will gain for you the world's friendship but will cut you off from God's friendship. Which means more

---

24. (a) Why is it unwise to become imitators of persons on whom the world bestows honor? (b) How can our attitude toward material possessions show whose friendship we are really seeking?

to you? Which will lead to greater and more enduring happiness?

²⁵ It is easy to give in to the world's pattern. And, because of its bad spirit, supporters of this world will resent it if you take a separate course. (1 Peter 4:3, 4) Pressures will be brought on you to conform, to let worldly human society mold you into its likeness. The world's wisdom—its philosophies as to what brings success in life—will be used to try to control your thinking. So, it takes real effort and faith to 'make your mind over' to see things from God's viewpoint and see why 'the wisdom of this world is foolishness in his sight.' (1 Corinthians 1:18-20; 2:14-16; 3:18-20) By diligent study of God's Word we can see through the world's false wisdom, see the bad results that it is already bringing, and the disastrous end to which it must lead. Then we can also come to appreciate fully the wisdom of God's way and the sure blessings that it guarantees.

USELESS TO GIVE LIFE AND ENERGIES TO A PASSING WORLD

²⁶ Some may object: 'But do not many of the organizations of the world do good, working for the protection, health, education and freedom of the people?' True, certain organizations do give some temporary relief from a few of the people's troubles. Yet they are all part of the world alienated from God, and they turn the people's attention toward perpetuating this present system of things. None of them are advocates of God's

---

25. (a) What should we expect from the world when we leave behind its ways? (b) What will enable us really to 'make our minds over' to view things as God does?
26. Would it be wise to get involved in the work of humanitarian organizations of the world with a view to improving conditions?

government for earth, his kingdom by his Son. After all, even some criminals who engage in vicious and harmful activities may raise families, provide for them and even do charitable works for the community. But would these things justify giving our support to criminal organizations in any way?—Compare 2 Corinthians 6:14-16.

27 Can we really show true love for mankind by associating ourselves with any of the world's schemes, devoting time and energy to make these succeed? If you wanted to help persons who were ill and diseased, would you do so by associating with them in such a way that you contracted their same ailments and diseases? Or would you not be of far greater aid to them if you stayed healthy yourself and tried to aid them to find the way to health? The present human society is spiritually sick and diseased. None of us can save it, for God's Word shows its sickness is leading to its death. (Compare Isaiah 1:4-9.) But we can help *individuals* in the world to find the way to spiritual health and to survival into a righteous new order—provided we ourselves maintain separateness from the world. (2 Corinthians 6:17) Wisely, then, shun involvement in the world's schemes, and exert yourself to avoid becoming infected by the spirit of the world and imitating its unrighteous ways. Never forget, the "world is passing away and so is its desire, but he that does the will of God remains forever."—1 John 2:17.

---

27. What is the only way that we can help people in this world to be among the survivors into God's new order?

CHAPTER 12

Respect for Authority
Essential for Peaceful Living

THERE is a spirit of independence that permeates the world in our day. Particularly among those born since World War II a general rejection of authority has developed. Why? For one thing, their parents had observed and experienced oppression on an unprecedented scale, as well as high-handed and corrupt tactics by those in power. They developed a dim view of authority. Consequently, many of them, on becoming parents, did not instill in their children a respect for authority. Nor have the injustices seen by the children helped matters. As a result, rebellion against authority has become common.

[2] That rebellion is expressed in various ways. Sometimes it is shown by adopting a type of dress that indicates rejection of "accepted standards." It may involve public defiance of the police, or even violence and bloodshed. But it is not limited to these. Even among persons who do not express themselves in these more open ways, how many are there who ignore or sidestep laws or other regulations if they do not agree with them or if they find it inconvenient to do what these require?

[3] This situation has deeply affected the atmosphere in homes, in schools, at places of employ-

1-3. (a) What has contributed to widespread rejection of authority in our day? (b) In what various ways is this attitude expressed? (c) Where are the effects felt?

ment and in contacts with government officials. More and more people just do not want anyone else to be telling them what to do. They are reaching out for what they believe to be greater freedom. Faced with this situation, what will you do?

⁴ Your course will unavoidably indicate where you stand in relation to the issue of the rightfulness of Jehovah's universal sovereignty. Do you really look to Jehovah as the Source of true peace and security? Will you seek out and apply in your life what his Word says? Or are you going along with those of mankind who, being misled by Satan, believe that they ought to make their own decisions as to what is good and what is bad? —Genesis 3:1-5; Revelation 12:9.

⁵ Anyone who allows what is "popular" to control his thinking will easily be misled. (Jeremiah 8:6) But an accurate knowledge of the Bible is a safeguard. It can protect you against simply exchanging one bad situation for another because of having listened to persons who, while 'promising freedom, are themselves existing as slaves of corruption.' Following the lead of such persons would only put you in the same enslaved condition. (2 Peter 2:18, 19) True freedom can be had only by learning and doing the will of God. His law is "the perfect law that belongs to freedom." (James 1:25) Jehovah does not needlessly restrict us, hedging us in with rules that serve no useful purpose. But he does provide the kind of guidance that enables a person to enjoy the peace and security that result from having a fine re-

---

4. By what we do in this matter, we show our attitude on what issue?
5. (a) What often results from following the lead of humans who promise "freedom"? (b) How free is the person who does God's will?

lationship with God and with one's fellowman. Is not that what you want?

⁶ Better than anyone else, God knows the extent to which there is corruption and misuse of authority in this old system of things. And he has given his word that, regardless of how highly situated those causing oppression may be, he will call them to account. (Romans 14:12) In God's appointed time, "the wicked . . . will be cut off from the very earth; and as for the treacherous, they will be torn away from it." (Proverbs 2:22) But it is not going to result in any lasting good for ourselves if we grow impatient and take the law into our own hands.—Romans 12:17-19.

⁷ On the night of his betrayal and arrest in the garden of Gethsemane, Jesus Christ emphasized this to his apostles. Because of the conditions in the land, including the presence of wild beasts, the Jews frequently carried weapons, and on that occasion there were two swords among Jesus' apostles. (Luke 22:38) What happened? Well, when they saw a violent distortion of justice— an effort to arrest Jesus without just cause and under cover of darkness—the apostle Peter impulsively drew his sword and struck off the ear of one of the men. But Jesus restored the severed ear and said to Peter: "Return your sword to its place, for all those who take the sword will perish by the sword." (Matthew 26:52) Many persons, even in our day, could have been saved from untimely deaths by following this advice.—Proverbs 24:21, 22.

6, 7. (a) Who is in the best position to do something about the misuse of authority in this system of things? (b) How did Jesus show what happens to persons who try to take the law into their own hands?

PROPER VIEW OF SECULAR AUTHORITY

[8] When writing to Christians in Rome, the apostle Paul was inspired by God to discuss how they were to conduct themselves in relation to secular authorities. He said: "Let every soul be in subjection to the superior authorities, for there is no authority except by God; the existing authorities stand placed in their relative positions by God. Therefore he who opposes the authority has taken a stand against the arrangement of God; those who have taken a stand against it will receive judgment to themselves." (Romans 13:1, 2) Does this mean that God has put these secular rulers in power? The Bible definitely answers, No! (Luke 4:5, 6; Revelation 13:1, 2) But they do exist by his permission, and the 'relative position' that they have occupied in the course of human history was determined by God. What has that position been?

[9] The scripture just quoted says that it is a "superior" one. Thus government officials are not to be treated with disrespect. The laws put into force by them are not to be disregarded. This does not necessarily mean that you admire the individuals, nor that you approve of any corruption in which they might engage. But respect is properly shown because of the office they occupy.—Titus 3:1, 2.

[10] In large measure, secular laws work for the good of the people. They help to maintain order and assure a measure of protection for the person and property of individuals. (Romans 13:3, 4)

8. (a) As stated at Romans 13:1, 2, how are Christians to view secular rulers? (b) What is meant by the statement that they are "placed in their relative positions by God"?
9. If officials engage in wrong practices, how can we respect them?
10. How is the payment of taxes to be viewed, and why?

Furthermore, the government usually provides roads, sanitation service, fire protection, education and other services that benefit the people. Are they to be paid for these services? Should we pay taxes? This is a question that is sometimes permeated with strong feelings because of the high tax rate and the frequent misuse of public funds. In the time of Jesus' earthly ministry, too, the question had political overtones. But Jesus did not take the position that the existing situation warranted any refusal to pay. Referring to the money that had been minted by the Roman Caesar, he said: "Pay back, therefore, Caesar's things to Caesar, but God's things to God." (Matthew 22:17-21; Romans 13:6, 7) Knowing the results that could easily develop, Jesus did not endorse the idea of each one becoming a law to himself.

[11] It is to be noted, however, that in his reply Jesus showed that the secular state was not the only authority to be considered. The "superior authorities" are not superior to God nor even equal to him. To the contrary, they "stand placed in their relative positions by God." (Romans 13:1) Their authority is limited, not absolute. Because of this, Christians have frequently been confronted with a critical decision. It is a decision that you too must make. When men in power demand for themselves what belongs to God, what will you do? If they forbid what God commands, whom will you obey?

[12] The apostles of Jesus Christ, choosing to uphold Jehovah's sovereignty, respectfully but

---

11, 12. (a) How do the scriptures under consideration show that there is also another authority to be considered? (b) What would you do if secular rulers issued orders that conflicted with God's requirements, and why?

firmly stated their position to the members of the high court in Jerusalem: "Whether it is righteous in the sight of God to listen to you rather than to God, judge for yourselves. But as for us, we cannot stop speaking about the things we have seen and heard. . . . We must obey God as ruler rather than men." (Acts 4:19, 20; 5:29) Political governments may impose restrictions on the number of people who may meet together; they may also prohibit certain public activity. God's Word does not require that his people assemble in *large* crowds for worship, nor does it say that there is only one proper way to contact other people to speak to them about God's will. On the other hand, if conforming to governmental restrictions were to make it impossible to fulfill God-given obligations, what then? Who can deny that the right thing to do would be to "obey God as ruler rather than men"?

[13] This is far different from independently doing what appeals to selfish interests instead of doing what the law requires. It is true that, from a personal standpoint, certain laws may seem unnecessary or unduly restrictive. But does that justify one's ignoring the law? What would be the result if everyone were to obey only the laws that he felt benefited himself? It would lead to anarchy.

[14] There is grave danger in a person's ignoring authority and doing only what pleases self simply because it is unlikely to result in immediate punishment. While such disregard for law may at first involve comparatively minor matters, a person's going unpunished may embolden him to

13, 14. (a) How careful should we be not to disobey secular laws just for personal reasons? (b) From the Scriptures, point out reasons for this.

greater lawlessness until he becomes set in his bad way. Regarding this, Ecclesiastes 8:11 states: "Because sentence against a bad work has not been executed speedily, that is why the heart of the sons of men has become fully set in them to do bad." What is the real reason for obeying the law? Should it be merely fear of punishment for disobeying? In the case of a Christian, there ought to be a far stronger inducement—what the apostle Paul referred to as a "compelling reason" —and that is the desire for a clean conscience. (Romans 13:5) When a person's conscience has been educated in harmony with the Scriptures, he knows that, if he were to pursue a lawless course, he would be taking a stand "against the arrangement of God." Regardless of whether other humans know what we are doing, God knows, and our prospects for future life depend on him. —1 Peter 2:12-17.

¹⁵ The same is true in regard to a young person's attitude toward his schoolteacher, and an adult's attitude toward his secular employer. The fact that many other people around us do wrong things should not be the determining factor. Whether the teacher or the employer knows what we do should not make any difference. The question is, What is right? What is pleasing to God? Schoolteachers are generally representatives of the secular government, agents of the "superior authorities," and so deserve respect. And as to secular employers, the Bible counsels: "Please them well, . . . exhibiting good fidelity to the full, so that [you] may adorn the teaching of our Savior, God, in all things." (Titus 2:9, 10) Doing

15. (a) What should guide a person in his attitude toward a schoolteacher or an employer? (b) In this way we avoid being influenced by whose spirit?

so, we show that we have not given in to the influence of Satan, whose spirit "operates in the sons of disobedience." Instead, we make a genuine contribution to peaceful relations with our fellowmen.—Ephesians 2:2, 3.

AUTHORITY WITHIN THE HOME

16 Another area in which peaceful relations are very much to be desired is the family circle. Too often such a wholesome relationship is lacking, resulting in a breakdown in family relations—in many cases, even the breaking up of the household. What can be done to improve the situation? A basic requirement is respect for Jehovah's arrangement of headship. As written at 1 Corinthians 11:3, that arrangement is as follows: "The head of every man is the Christ; in turn the head of a woman is the man; in turn the head of the Christ is God."

17 Notice that the statement begins with man's position, not pointing first to his headship, but, rather, drawing attention to the fact that, in Jehovah's arrangement of things, there is someone to whom the man should be looking for direction, someone whose example he should be following. Christ is the head of man, and in his dealings with his congregation, which is likened to a bride, Christ has demonstrated the way to make a success of husbandly headship. His fine example stirs a willing response in his followers. Instead of being a boss, harsh and demanding toward them, Jesus has been "mild-tempered and lowly in heart," so that his followers have found

16. What requirement for harmonious family life is stated at 1 Corinthians 11:3?
17. (a) As to headship, what is the man's position? (b) What fine example as to husbandly headship did Christ set?

refreshment for their souls. (Matthew 11:28-30) Has he belittled them for their shortcomings? To the contrary, he laid down his life to cleanse them of sins. (Ephesians 5:25-30) What a blessing to any household to have a man who sincerely endeavors to follow that example!

18 When there is such headship in the home, it is not difficult for a woman to look up to her husband. And obedience of the children to their parents comes more readily. But there is much that the wife and children too can contribute to the happiness of the family. By diligence in caring for the household, also by accepting her husband's decisions and working to make them succeed, a wife gives evidence that she truly does have "deep respect for her husband." Is that true in your household? (Ephesians 5:33; Proverbs 31:10-15, 27, 28) As for the children, if there is willing obedience to both father and mother, this shows that they honor their parents, and that is what God requires. (Ephesians 6:1-4) Do you not agree that there would be far more peace, and a much greater feeling of personal security, in such a household than in one where respect for authority is lacking?

19 You can help to make your home such a place. Whether other members of the family choose to uphold Jehovah's ways or not, you can do so. Others in the family may respond to your fine example. (1 Corinthians 7:16; Titus 2:6-8) Even if they do not, still what you do will stand as a demonstration of your faith in the rightness

---

18. (a) In what ways can a wife show that she respects the authority of her husband? (b) How are children to show respect for their parents, and why?

19. If you are the only one in the family who tries to be guided by God's Word, then what?

of God's ways, and that is something of no little value.—1 Peter 3:16, 17.

²⁰ Keep in mind that the entire framework of family authority has its origin with God. So, he cannot be left out of account, can he? Thus wives are instructed to be in subjection to their husbands "as it is becoming in the Lord." And children are counseled to be obedient to their parents "for this is well-pleasing in the Lord." (Colossians 3:18, 20) This means that the authority of a husband over his wife and of parents over their children is a relative one. If the husband or the parents are unbelievers, that idea might at first displease them. But really it works for their good, because it will help to make the believer more dependable and more respectful.

²¹ Of course, if a husband were to demand that his wife do something that would not be "becoming in the Lord," what she does will demonstrate whether she really does "fear the true God" or not. (Ecclesiastes 12:13) Likewise, when children are old enough to understand and obey God's Word, if their parents do not share their desire to serve Jehovah, the children must decide whether they will prove their loyalty to God or share the lot of parents who do not. Their prospects for eternal life are involved. (Matthew 10:37-39) Nevertheless, aside from their prior obligation to God, such children should be submissive in "everything," even if it means doing things that are not to their liking. (Colossians 3:20) Doing this, they may be able to help their parents, too,

20, 21. (a) How does the Bible show that the authority of a husband and of parents is not absolute? (b) So, with what decision may a Christian wife or believing children be faced, and what should motivate them?

to accept Jehovah's provisions for salvation. When one's motivation is, not disobedience born of an independent spirit, but loyalty to Jehovah and his righteous ways, this is truly "well-pleasing in the Lord."

IN THE CHRISTIAN CONGREGATION

[22] That same spirit of loyalty to Jehovah should be reflected in our attitude toward his Christian congregation and those who are caring for its interests. In the congregation Jehovah has provided overseers to shepherd the "flock." They receive no salary for their work, but, rather, give of themselves because of genuine concern for the welfare of their Christian brothers and sisters. (1 Thessalonians 2:8, 9) They help the congregation to carry out the special work entrusted to it, namely, the preaching of the good news of God's kingdom. Also, with concern for the individual welfare of the members of the congregation, they assist these to learn how to apply the principles of the Bible in their daily lives. Further, if any member of the congregation, though knowing what God requires, deliberately persists in serious wrongdoing, the responsible overseers see that he is expelled, and thus the rest of the congregation is protected from his corrupting influence.—1 Corinthians 5:12, 13.

[23] In appreciation for this loving provision of Jehovah to assure a spirit of peacefulness among his people, we should heed the admonition found at Hebrews 13:17, namely: "Be obedient to those who are taking the lead among you and be sub-

22, 23. (a) What do Christian overseers do on behalf of the members of the congregation? (b) So, what attitude does Hebrews 13:17 say that we should have toward them?

missive, for they are keeping watch over your souls as those who will render an account; that they may do this with joy and not with sighing, for this would be damaging to you."

[24] Rendering obedience to "those who are taking the lead," however, does not mean becoming mere men pleasers. The Bible emphasizes that a principal reason why these overseers or elders deserve respect is because what they are teaching is "the word of God." (Hebrews 13:7; 1 Timothy 5:17) And concerning that word, Hebrews 4:12, 13 states: "The word of God is alive and exerts power and is sharper than any two-edged sword and pierces even to the dividing of soul and spirit, and of joints and their marrow, and is able to discern thoughts and intentions of the heart. And there is not a creation that is not manifest to his sight, but all things are naked and openly exposed to the eyes of him with whom we have an accounting."

[25] That "word of God" truly reveals what a person is inside. It exposes the difference between what he may appear to be and the dominant attitude that moves him to speak and act as he does. If he really has faith in God, and is motivated by a genuine desire to please his Creator, he will not lapse into wrongdoing when out of sight of the elders of the congregation. Nor will he engage in some unscriptural conduct simply because it is not among the serious wrongs for which a person would be expelled from the congregation. His desire is, not to sin, but properly to reflect "the glory of God." (Romans 3:23) On the

24, 25. (a) How should what the elders teach influence the way we view them? (b) When and where should we apply what we are taught from the Bible? Why?

other hand, if anyone is inclined to take lightly any of the counsel found in God's Word, he ought to examine carefully what his attitude toward God really is. Is he becoming like that person concerning whom Psalm 14:1 [13:1, *Dy*] says: "The senseless one has said"—no, not publicly—but "in his heart: 'There is no Jehovah' "?

²⁶ When tempted by the Devil, Jesus Christ firmly declared: "Man must live . . . on every utterance coming forth through Jehovah's mouth." (Matthew 4:4) Do you feel that strongly about the matter? Do you believe that "every utterance" of Jehovah is important and that none are to be ignored? Obeying some of Jehovah's requirements, while treating others as unimportant, simply is not enough. Either we uphold the rightfulness of Jehovah's sovereignty or we take the Devil's side of the issue by setting our own standard of what is good and what is bad. Happy are those who show that they truly love Jehovah's law.—Psalm 119:165 [118:165, *Dy*].

²⁷ Such persons are not ensnared by the divisive spirit of the world. Nor do they indulge in the shameful conduct of those who throw off moral restraint. Deep respect for Jehovah and his righteous ways gives stability to their lives.

26, 27. (a) Why is it important to take seriously "every utterance" of Jehovah? (b) How are our lives affected when we thus show respect for authority?

CHAPTER 13

Your View of Sex
—What Difference Does It Make?

THERE are people who have the opinion that the Bible disapproves of everything that has to do with sex. That, of course, is not what the Bible itself says. After telling about God's creation of the first man and woman, the Bible goes on to relate: "God blessed them and God said to them: 'Be fruitful and become many and fill the earth.'"—Genesis 1:27, 28.

² Sexual relations between man and woman therefore have divine approval. But are they to be indulged in without limitations? Would such a view result in our gaining the greatest enjoyment from life? Would it bring true peace and security for ourselves and for those around us?

³ Sex is just as subject to misuse as are other human functions. Eating is good and essential for life; yet gluttony can impair health and shorten one's life. Sleep, too, is vital; but an excess robs life of accomplishment, and can even weaken the body. Just as real enjoyment of life does not result from gluttony, drunkenness and laziness, so, too, it does not result from unrestrained use of one's sexual powers. Human experience for thousands of years bears testimony to this. Must we find it out through bitter personal experience? There is a better way.

1-3. (a) How does the Bible show that sexual relations between man and woman have divine approval? (b) Would it be for a person's good to indulge in unrestrained use of his sexual powers?

145

[4] God's Word gives a balanced view of sex that will protect our happiness now and in the future. Yet, not just for the sake of our own peace and security, but, more importantly, out of respect for our Creator, we should seek to learn and hold to his standards concerning the use of these faculties with which he endowed mankind. Do we truly place ourselves on his side in the issue involving the rightness of his rulership? Then in this matter too we will gladly submit to his superior wisdom and authority as the Universal Sovereign.—Jeremiah 10:10, 23.

KEEPING MARRIAGE HONORABLE AMONG ALL

[5] The Bible exhorts: "Let marriage be honorable among all, and the marriage bed be without defilement, for God will judge fornicators and adulterers." (Hebrews 13:4) So, God is against persons who engage in sexual relations outside of marriage. This is consistent with the fact that, when providing the first man with a mate, God showed that his will was for a man and his wife to become "one flesh," in a lasting bond of union. Some four thousand years later, God's Son showed that his Father had not abandoned this standard. (Genesis 2:22-24; Matthew 19:4-6) But is such a standard needlessly restrictive? Does it deprive us of something good? Let us see.

[6] Adultery violates the divine standard, and Jehovah God promises to become "a speedy witness" in judgment against adulterers. (Malachi 3:5) The bad fruits of sexual relations with someone outside the marriage union emphasize the

4. What should motivate us to uphold God's standards regarding sex?
5. What does the Bible say about engaging in any sexual relations outside of marriage?
6. What shows that God's law against adultery is for our good?

wisdom of God's law. Adultery produces broken confidence and distrust. It causes insecurity and undermines marital peace. The resulting bitterness and heartbreak often lead to divorce. Children suffer as they see their family torn apart. Considering these things, do you not agree that God's condemnation of adultery is for our good? His Word shows that anyone having genuine love of neighbor will not commit adultery.—Romans 13:8-10.

[7] As we have observed, the Bible also expresses God's judgment against fornicators. Exactly what is "fornication"? While the Bible's use of this term can include sexual intercourse on the part of unmarried persons as well as adultery, it has a much broader meaning. The word for "fornication" that is used when recording the statements of Jesus and his disciples is the Greek word *por-nei'a*. It is drawn from the same root word as the modern term "pornography." *Por-nei'a* was used in Bible times to describe all forms of unlawful sexual intercourse. (*The Vocabulary of the Greek New Testament,* by Moulton and Milligan) It includes not only ordinary sexual relations between persons who are not married to each other, but also perverted sexual relations between such persons. Thus another reference work states that *por-nei'a* "can also be 'unnatural vice,' . . . sodomy."[36]

[8] When urging his Christian brothers to "abstain from fornication," the apostle Paul gave strong reasons for their doing so, saying: "That no one go to the point of harming and encroach

7. Explain what is meant by "fornication," as referred to in the Bible.
8. For what strong reasons did the apostle Paul urge Christians to "abstain from fornication"?

upon the rights of his brother in this matter, because Jehovah is one who exacts punishment for all these things . . . For God called us, not with allowance for uncleanness . . . So, then, the man that shows disregard is disregarding, not man, but God."—1 Thessalonians 4:3-8.

⁹ One committing fornication does indeed 'harm and encroach upon the rights of others.' This is true, for example, of persons who live with one of the opposite sex without benefit of legal marriage. Why do they do it? Frequently it is so that they can abandon the union whenever they please. They do not give their partner in such an arrangement any of the security that responsible marriage ought to bring. But what if both persons engage in fornication willingly, with mutual agreement? Are they still 'harming and encroaching on the rights of others'? Yes, definitely so.

¹⁰ For one thing, anyone participating in fornication shares in damaging the other person's conscience as well as any clean standing with God. The fornicator also destroys the other person's opportunity to enter marriage with a clean start. He likely brings disrespect, reproach and distress on members of the other person's family, as well as his own. He may also endanger the mental, emotional and physical health of the other person. Dread venereal diseases are frequently linked with such sexual immorality. While the guilt for any such harm rests most heavily on the one who promoted the fornication, nevertheless, both parties share in that guilt.

9, 10. (a) Frequently, why does a person hold back from legal marriage, even though living with someone of the opposite sex? (b) Even if the fornication is by mutual agreement, how is there 'harm and an encroaching on the rights of others'?

¹¹ Passionate desire may cause persons to choose to blind themselves to these harms. But do you believe that God, in his righteousness, will pass over or condone such callous disregard for the rights of others? God's Word calls for loving one's neighbor as oneself and for 'honoring,' not debasing or repudiating, his sacred marriage arrangement.—Matthew 22:39; Hebrews 13:4.

¹² What of homosexuality? As we have seen, this practice is covered by the word *por·nei'a* ("fornication"), used by Jesus and his disciples. The disciple Jude used that word when referring to the unnatural sex acts of the men of Sodom and Gomorrah. (Jude 7) Homosexuality there caused degradation that produced a loud "cry of complaint" and led to God's destruction of those cities and their inhabitants. (Genesis 18:20; 19:23, 24) Has God's view changed since then? No. First Corinthians 6:9, 10, for example, lists "men who lie with men" among those who, if continuing such a practice, will not inherit God's kingdom. Also, describing the results to persons who 'dishonor their bodies in uncleanness,' going after "flesh for unnatural use," the apostle Paul writes that they "became violently inflamed in their lust toward one another, males with males, working what is obscene and receiving in themselves the full recompense, which was due for their error." (Romans 1:24, 27) Not only do such persons fall under God's condemnation. They also receive a "recompense" of mental and physical corruption. Today, for example, there is much syphilis among homosexuals. The high standard

11. Why is there no reason for anyone to believe that God will condone fornication?
12. (a) What shows God's view of homosexuality? (b) Against what does God's law forbidding homosexuality protect us?

set out in God's Word, rather than depriving us of something good, protects us against such harm.

ACCEPTING GOD'S VIEW OF DIVORCE

[13] "I hate divorce." That is the way Jehovah God expressed his strong feeling when reproving those who 'dealt treacherously' with their marriage mates. (Malachi 2:14-16, *Revised Standard Version*) His Word supplies abundant counsel to aid persons to make a success of marriage and to avoid the bitterness of divorce. It also makes clear that God views faithfulness to one's marriage vows as a sacred responsibility.

[14] This is emphasized by the fact that he acknowledges only one proper basis for divorce. His Son showed what this is: "I say to you that whoever divorces his wife, except on the ground of fornication [*por·nei′a*], and marries another commits adultery." (Matthew 19:9; 5:32) *Por·nei′a*, as we have seen, refers to all immoral sexual intercourse outside of marriage, whether natural or unnatural.

[15] If one's mate becomes guilty of such "fornication" today, does this automatically break the marriage tie? No, the innocent mate can decide whether to forgive or not. Where divorce is decided upon, the Christian's recognition of the proper authority of secular government will cause him to dissolve the marriage legally, doing so on a truthful, legal basis. (Romans 13:1, 2) When the proceedings are finalized, remarriage is allowable. But the Scriptures counsel that any such mar-

13. How serious is the matter of faithfulness to one's marriage vows?
14, 15. (a) What is the only proper basis for divorce? (b) Does such "fornication" automatically break the marriage tie? (c) Under what circumstances is remarriage allowable?

riage should be only to another Christian, one who is really "in the Lord."—1 Corinthians 7:39.

[16] What if the laws of a land do not allow *any* divorce, even on the ground of sexual immorality? An innocent mate in such case might be able to obtain a divorce in a country where divorce is permitted. Circumstances, of course, may not make this possible. But some form of legal separation may be available in one's own country and could then be sought. Whichever the case, the innocent mate could separate from the guilty one and present definite proof of Scriptural grounds for divorce to the elders who serve in a judicial capacity in the local congregation of Jehovah's Christian witnesses. Then if that one were later to decide to take another mate, the congregation would not act to remove him as an adulterer from the congregation, provided a written statement is filed with the congregation. This statement must contain a vow of faithfulness to the present mate and agreement to obtain a legal marriage certificate if the estranged legal mate should die. Nevertheless, the individual would have to face whatever consequences this might result in for him as far as the world outside the congregation is concerned. For the world does not generally recognize that God's law is superior to human laws and that such human laws have only relative authority. —Compare Acts 5:29.

WISELY AVOIDING ALL UNCLEANNESS AND SEXUAL GREED

[17] Sexual relations plainly have a proper place

16. In lands where secular law does not allow for divorce on any basis whatsoever, how do Jehovah's Christian witnesses show due respect for God's law on the matter?
17. From the Scriptures, explain the proper place that sexual relations have in the lives of married persons.

in the lives of married persons. God provided this as the means by which children would be produced, as also a source of pleasurable satisfaction to the parents. (Genesis 9:1; Proverbs 5:18, 19; 1 Corinthians 7:3-5) Nevertheless, he warned against abusing this gift.

[18] Because of the emphasis placed on sex in modern society, many young folks find that their desire for sexual satisfaction is aroused even before they are in position to marry. As a result, some of them seek pleasure through self-stimulation of their sexual parts. This is masturbation or self-abuse. Is it a proper or wise thing to do?

[19] The Scriptures counsel: "Deaden, therefore, your body members that are upon the earth as respects fornication, uncleanness, sexual appetite, hurtful desire, and covetousness." (Colossians 3:5) Is one who practices masturbation 'deadening his body members as respects sexual appetite'? To the contrary, he is stimulating the sexual appetite. He develops a craving for activity that is not yet proper for him, so he satisfies the craving in an unclean way. (Ephesians 4:19) The Bible urges that one avoid the kind of thinking and conduct that leads to such problems, that he replace it with wholesome activity, and that he cultivate self-control. (Philippians 4:8; Galatians 5:22, 23) When earnest effort is put forth to do this, such self-abuse can be avoided, with benefits mentally, emotionally and spiritually to the individual.

18, 19. (a) Why is the practice of masturbation or self-abuse not proper for a Christian? (b) What can aid a person to avoid such a practice?

[20] What the Bible says respecting "uncleanness, sexual appetite, hurtful desire" applies to all Christians, single and married. It is true that husband and wife have a Scriptural and legal right to engage in sexual relations with each other, and to enjoy doing so. But does this mean that they can throw off all restraint? The fact that God's Word urges all Christians to cultivate self-control argues against such a view. (2 Peter 1:5-8) The inspired Bible writer did not have to explain to married persons the natural way in which the reproductive organs of husband and wife complement each other. Homosexual relations obviously cannot follow this natural way. So, male and female homosexuals employ other forms of intercourse in what the apostle refers to as the satisfying of "disgraceful sexual appetites" and "obscene" practices. (Romans 1:24-32) Is it reasonable that married couples could imitate such homosexual forms of intercourse in their own marriage relations and still be free in God's eyes from expressing "disgraceful sexual appetites" or "hurtful desire"?

[21] On considering what the Scriptures say, a person may realize that his former thinking on these matters was molded by persons who are, as the Bible says, "past all moral sense." But a change can be made. With God's help, one can "put on the new personality," which is molded in accord with true righteousness. (Ephesians 4:17-24) In this way he shows that he truly means it when he says that he wants to do God's will.

20. What shows that it would not be proper for husband and wife to throw off all restraint in their sexual relations with each other?
21. Regardless of what a person's way of life may have been in the past, what opportunity is open to him now?

YOUR VIEW VITALLY AFFECTS
YOUR PEACE AND SECURITY

[22] Really, applying the counsel of God's Word as respects sexual morality is not burdensome. Contrast the fruitage of the course the Bible outlines with the world's high rate of divorce, its broken homes, delinquent children, its prostitution, and the violence and murders committed in connection with sexual passion. (Proverbs 7:10, 25-27) How evident the wisdom of God's Word! By rejecting worldly thinking based on selfish desire and greed, and by bringing your thinking into harmony with Jehovah's counsel, your heart will be greatly strengthened in right desires. In place of fleeting pleasures of sexual immorality, you will enjoy a clean conscience and enduring peace of mind. Marriage and family ties will be fortified with the growth of mutual trust between marriage mates and of respect by their children.

[23] And do not lose sight of the fact that your very hope of eternal life is involved. Scriptural morality will contribute to more than your present health. (Proverbs 5:3-11) It will become part of the evidence that you truly deplore the detestable things done by people who hypocritically profess to believe in God and that you have been 'marked' for survival into God's "new earth," where righteousness is to dwell. How vital, then, that you 'do your utmost now to be found finally by God spotless and unblemished and in peace.'—Ezekiel 9:4-6; 2 Peter 3:11-14.

22. What immediate benefits come to those who apply the counsel of God's Word in regard to sexual morality?
23. How is one's view of sex a factor in his being 'marked' for survival into God's "new earth"?

CHAPTER 14

Respect for the Gift of Life

DEEP respect for the gift of life is a foundation of true peace and security. But such respect is sadly lacking among many people. As is well known, men can take away life by killing; but no man can restore life once it is gone.

² We should show respect for life as a sacred obligation. To whom? To the Giver of life, the one to whom the psalmist said: "For with you," namely, Jehovah God, "is the source of life." (Psalm 36:9 [35:10, *Dy*]) We owe our lives to him, not only because he created man, but also because he has allowed mankind to continue reproducing till now and has provided the means for sustaining life. (Acts 14:16, 17) More than that, he caused his Son to become the Repurchaser or Redeemer of the human family, buying it with his own precious lifeblood. (Romans 5:6-8; Ephesians 1:7) As a result, he now extends to all who will accept it the grand hope of life in his righteous new order. That is something that we really want, is it not? In view of all this, should we not deeply respect and appreciate God's gift of life? How can we do so?

³ For one thing, if we are serious about showing respect for life, we will not join with those who, simply for entertainment, feed their minds on programs that feature violence. Accepting violence as "entertaining" has caused many to become

---

1, 2. Why should we show deep respect for the gift of life?
3. How does one's watching violence for entertainment affect his attitude toward life?

hardened and unfeeling toward human suffering and loss of life. They learn to live just for the present and show little concern for their own or anyone else's future welfare. But if we are grateful for God's goodness and the hope he gives, we will resist such spirit. We will cultivate appreciation for life as a gift from God. This will affect how we use our own lives, how we treat other people, even how we view those who have not yet been born.

RESPECTING THE LIFE OF THE UNBORN

⁴ The power to pass on life is a grand privilege, divinely given. That life is passed on, not at birth, but at the time of conception. As the *Encyclopædia Britannica* states, it is then that "the life-history of the individual, as a distinct and biological entity begins."[37] Similarly, God's interest in a human life begins before birth. The psalmist David wrote, saying to God: "You kept me screened off in the belly of my mother. . . . Your eyes saw *even the embryo of me,* and in your book all its parts were down in writing."—Psalm 139:13-16 [138:13-16, *Dy*]; Ecclesiastes 11:5.

⁵ In modern times the lives of millions of unborn children are deliberately being ended by abortion. Is this right? Some argue that the unborn baby has no conscious appreciation of what life is and is incapable of a separate existence outside the womb. But that is also basically true of a newborn baby. At birth it has no grasp of life's meaning, nor could it continue existence apart from constant care of parents or others. The living cell

4. (a) When is life passed on to one's offspring? (b) What shows whether God is interested in a human life before birth?
5. Why are the arguments put forth in an effort to justify abortion not sound?

formed in the womb at the time of conception has
every possibility of becoming a baby if not inter-
fered with. Taking the life of a newborn baby is
viewed as a crime nearly everywhere. Even where
babies are born prematurely, great effort is made
to save them. Why, then, should it not also be
viewed as a crime for anyone to take the life of
the unborn to prevent its further development and
birth? Why should life be viewed as sacred only
after it leaves the womb and not also while inside
the womb?

⁶ The important thing is not just how men may
view matters but what God, the Giver of life, says.
To Jehovah God the life of the unborn child is
precious, not to be trifled with. He gave a law
to ancient Israel specifically protecting the life
of the unborn child. If, in a struggle between two
men, a pregnant woman was injured or a mis-
carriage resulted, this law set forth strict pen-
alties. (Exodus 21:22, 23) Manifestly the deliberate taking of the life of an unborn child would
be even more serious. According to God's law,
whenever human life was taken deliberately, the
guilty one was sentenced to death as a murderer.
(Numbers 35:30, 31) God maintains the same
high regard for life now.

⁷ Deep respect for God's will regarding the life
of the unborn child works to real benefit. By his
making parents fully responsible for the life of
the unborn, he provides a curb to sexual pro-
miscuity with all its bad effects—venereal disease,
unwanted pregnancies, illegitimate children,
broken families and the mental strain of an un-

6. How does the Bible indicate God's view toward the deliberate
taking of the life of an unborn child?
7. Against what are we protected when we respect God's will
regarding the life of an unborn child?

clean conscience. This can contribute to family peace now and is an important factor in our gaining future blessings.

RESPECT FOR YOUR OWN LIFE

[8] What about the way you treat your own body, what you do with your own life? Some persons say, 'I didn't choose to be born. So what I do with my life is up to me. I'll do whatever I want.' But must a gift be requested for the receiver to appreciate it? Life itself is undeniably good; it is only the badness of men and human imperfection that rob life of much of its joy. Jehovah God is not to blame for this; he promises to correct it by his Kingdom government. So, while we live we should do so in a way that shows respect for his will and purpose.—Romans 12:1.

[9] One way that we can show such appreciation is by moderation in food and drink. Gluttony and drunkenness are condemned by God. (Proverbs 23:20, 21) On the other hand, just as eating in moderation is proper so is the use of alcoholic beverages in moderation. This is shown by many scriptures.—Deuteronomy 14:26; Isaiah 25:6; Luke 7:33, 34; 1 Timothy 5:23.

[10] So, it is not drinking but drunkenness that is condemned in the Bible. And with good reason. Drunkenness damages the body, makes persons act stupidly and can even make them a danger to others. (Proverbs 23:29-35; Ephesians 5:18) It can shorten life, often leading to cirrhosis of the liver. In the United States alone, where per-

8. Why should we show respect for God's will in the way we treat our own body?
9. What does the Bible say about gluttony and drunkenness?
10. (a) How does a drunkard show disrespect for life? (b) As shown at 1 Corinthians 6:9, 10, why is it important to avoid drunkenness?

haps nine million persons show some form of alcoholism, the total loss each year in potential wages, accidents, medical care and crime is estimated at upwards of 750 million dollars. The cost in broken homes, ruined lives and human suffering is "beyond calculation." (*The Pharmacological Basis of Therapeutics,* 1970, p. 291) It is not surprising, therefore, that the apostle Paul says: "Do not be misled. Neither fornicators, . . . nor drunkards, nor revilers, nor extortioners will inherit God's kingdom."—1 Corinthians 6:9, 10.

[11] True, some feel keenly the depressing effect of the world situation. Its wars, crime, inflation and poverty, its stress and pressures contribute to nagging personal problems. But nothing is gained by trying to escape this through harmful excesses. These only create more problems for oneself and for others and, in the process, destroy one's dignity and purpose in living.

USE OF DRUGS

[12] In their endeavor to escape from the problems of life, increasing numbers of people are turning to drugs. Of course, many drugs have a medical use. Persons who are sick may need to use them to aid in recovery from illness. But what of the use of drugs where no treatment for illness is involved, where the user simply desires to get a dreamy feeling or even to go into a sort of trance? How is the life of the user affected?

[13] Today many persons who seek these pleasures use such "hard" drugs as heroin and cocaine, or they use so-called "psychedelic" drugs such as

---

11. Is it sensible to try to escape from personal problems by excessive drinking?
12. Why do many persons turn to the use of drugs?
13. What effects do some of these drugs have on the user, and so what do Bible principles indicate as to using them?

LSD. Some take large doses of amphetamine and barbiturate pills. What is the result? Their use of these drugs easily leads to loss of self-control, producing effects similar to those seen in a drunk person. (1 Corinthians 6:9, 10; Proverbs 23:33) It is generally recognized, even by most users, that these drugs can be dangerous. In New York city, for example, heroin addiction is the leading cause of death among persons between the ages of 18 and 35. What gross disregard for the gift of life!

[14] But what of the use of marijuana (marihuana), generally viewed as a nonaddictive drug? It, too, can be dangerous in several ways. One way is noted in a folder published by the U.S. Department of Health, Education, and Welfare. It explains that "users of one illicit drug may be exposed to a variety of them through contacts with drug sellers and other users." Likewise a report published in the *U.S. News & World Report* of February 1, 1971, under the heading, "Latest Findings on Marijuana," says that "there is evidence that people who have come to lean on the drug for psychological reasons—in the belief it will relieve tension and depression—are likely to go on to stronger drugs."

[15] But even if this does not happen, the smoking of marijuana itself can be dangerous. While views differ somewhat, it is noteworthy that one investigation revealed this: "Sufficiently high doses . . . can cause unpredictable, acute—although temporary—psychotic episodes manifesting themselves in the form of illusions, hallucinations, paranoia, depression and panic."[38] This same re-

14, 15. Although marijuana is generally viewed as nonaddictive, why are those who smoke it not showing real respect for the gift of life?

port also says that continued regular use of marijuana can cause adverse physical effects such as "liver damage, genetic defects, brain damage and upper respiratory ailment." In view of such possible risks, is one who uses marijuana showing respect for the gift of life?

[16] There is another powerful reason for avoiding the use of drugs to get a false sense of well-being. They can open the way for a person to come under the control of the demons. Many drug users themselves acknowledge that the use of drugs often is accompanied with involvement in occult practices. This linking of drugs with occultism is by no means new. Sorcerers in the past employed drugs. Vine's *Expository Dictionary of New Testament Words* observes: "In sorcery, the use of drugs, whether simple or potent, was generally accompanied by incantations and appeals to occult powers . . . to impress the applicant with the mysterious resources and powers of the sorcerer." These comments are made in connection with the Greek word rendered "practice of spiritism" (*phar·ma·ki'a*, literally "druggery") at Galatians 5:20. (See also Revelation 9:21; 18:23.) So today, as in times past, drugs can expose one to demon influence. How could anyone who wants to be a loyal servant of Jehovah expose himself to such danger simply for a momentary feeling of exhilaration?

[17] As is well known, drug use is inseparably linked with crime and the moral breakdown in society. Illicit drug sales are a major source of

---

16. To what other serious danger can the use of drugs expose a person, and how should this affect our view on the matter?
17, 18. (a) What other bad fruitage has become associated with drug use? (b) So, how do Jehovah's Christian witnesses view the use of drugs?

income for organized crime. A large percentage of drug addicts commit thefts and burglaries to support their habit. Others turn to prostitution. Families by the thousands are torn apart when a member becomes an addict. Pregnant mothers pass on addiction to their babies, who sometimes die while undergoing the agonies of withdrawal. And in most lands the possession and use of such dangerous drugs for nonmedical reasons is illegal.—Matthew 22:17-21.

[18] Do you want to have anything to do with a practice that is associated with all of that bad fruitage? Jehovah's Christian witnesses do not! They want no part of the use of drugs for thrills or to flee from reality. They have a high regard for life and want to use their lives in a way that is consistent with God's will.

USE OF TOBACCO AND SIMILAR PRODUCTS

[19] Even more common today is the use of tobacco and, in some lands, betel nut and the leaves of the coca plant. Though used by millions around the world, each of these is known to be damaging to the body and, in some cases, the mind. Tobacco has been the object of government warnings of its connection with such diseases as lung cancer, heart ailments, chronic bronchitis and emphysema. Does it show respect for the gift of life to use such addictive and harmful products?

[20] One might say that these things are all God's creation. True, but so are mushrooms, yet some

19. Why does respect for the gift of life enter into one's view toward use of tobacco, betel nut and the leaves of the coca plant? 20, 21. (a) Does the fact that the Bible does not condemn such habits by name mean that they are all right? (b) What Bible principles show that such habits have no place in the life of a person who is serious about wanting to do the will of God?

varieties are fatal to man if eaten. Another might say that the Bible does not specifically mention or condemn such habits. No, but, as we have seen, there are many things not specifically condemned in the Bible that are obviously wrong. The Bible nowhere specifically forbids using the backyard of one's neighbor as a place for dumping garbage. Yet the command to "love your neighbor as yourself" should be enough for any of us to recognize how wrong that would be.—Matthew 22:39.

[21] At 2 Corinthians 7:1 God's Word tells us to "cleanse ourselves of every defilement of flesh and spirit, perfecting holiness in God's fear." For something to be "holy" means for it to be "bright, clean, untarnished, uncorrupted." Jehovah God keeps himself clean and free from corruption, never lowering himself to act in an unholy manner. Rightly God expects us to continue "perfecting holiness" to the extent possible for us humans. (Romans 12:1) Also, he expects us to 'love him with our whole heart, soul, mind and strength,' but how can anyone do this if he indulges in practices that defile his body, damage his health and shorten his life?—Mark 12:29, 30.

[22] Though one or another of such habits may seem to have a 'stranglehold' on a person, he can overcome it and gain freedom. Knowledge of God and of his grand purposes provides a powerful motivation for doing so. A person can 'be made new in the force actuating his mind.' (Ephesians 4:23) This will open up a new way of life, one that results in personal contentment and is an honor to God.

22. What can enable a person to break the hold that such a bad habit may have on him?

RESPECT FOR LIFE AS REPRESENTED
BY BLOOD

[23] Our blood, too, deserves consideration when we speak of life. God has made blood, both of man and of animals, the symbol of life. This is shown in the law he gave to Noah and his sons, from whom we all descend, and in his later law to the nation of Israel. The only use of blood there approved by God was in the sacrifices offered up on the altar in accord with his instructions. (Genesis 9:3, 4; Leviticus 17:10-14) Those sacrifices all pictured the one sacrifice of God's own Son, by which he poured out his lifeblood on behalf of mankind. (Hebrews 9:11-14) This in itself should cause us to give careful attention to God's will in this matter.

[24] Is God's restriction regarding the use of blood still in force for true Christians? Yes, as is shown by the official statement made by the apostles and other elders of the Christian congregation in the first century. Under guidance of God's spirit, they wrote: "The holy spirit and we ourselves have favored adding no further burden to you, except these necessary things, to keep abstaining from things sacrificed to idols and from blood and from things strangled [hence, unbled] and from fornication. If you carefully keep yourselves from these things, you will prosper."—Acts 15:28, 29.

[25] But today many persons show complete disregard for God's will regarding this vital element of life. They use blood indiscriminately in food,

23. (a) What is the only use of blood that God approved in his law to Israel? (b) Why should the meaning of those sacrifices cause us to consider carefully God's will in this matter?
24. What does Acts 15:28, 29 say as to the view that Christians should have toward use of blood?
25. By what practices does the world show disregard for God's will regarding blood?

for medical purposes, even as an ingredient in commercial products, including fertilizer. Yet, is this not characteristic of a world where there is so much disregard for the gift of life itself? If we, however, sincerely appreciate life and our accountability to God, we will not ignore his will or insult him by violation of his express commands.

26 Thus, though we should be concerned over our health and seek to protect our lives as a gift from God, even here there are certain limits to observe. God's Son made this clear when he said: "He that is fond of his soul [or, life] destroys it, but he that hates his soul in this world will safeguard it for everlasting life."—John 12:25.

27 What does that mean? It means that, if it is a question of facing death because of obeying God or of disobeying him to preserve one's present life, the true servant of God would prefer death to disobedience. By disobeying God, Jesus Christ himself could have escaped death by impalement, but he did not. And men before him had shown the same unbreakable devotion to God's will. (Matthew 26:38, 39, 51-54; Hebrews 11:32-38) They did not let their present life stand in the way of their qualifying for life everlasting.

28 Is that the way that you, too, view life? Do you appreciate that, for life to have real meaning, you must live it in harmony with the will of God? Cultivating that viewpoint now is part of preparation for life in God's new order. How secure and safe one will then feel, anywhere and at any time, knowing that all those living on earth have genuine respect for God's gift of life.

26, 27. Why would efforts to preserve one's present life by disobeying God not show genuine respect for God's gift of life?
28. By cultivating appreciation for the Bible's view toward life, for what are we preparing?

CHAPTER 15

Why Care What Happens to Other People?

UNSELFISH concern about the welfare of others is rare today. It is true that all of us are born with the capacity to love. But when a person finds that others try to take unfair advantage of him, or his own efforts to show love are misunderstood, he may conclude that the best course is simply to look out for himself. Other people, seeing that those who exploit their fellowman for selfish advantage often prosper materially, may think that this is the way to succeed. The result is that most people have very few real friends, if any. There is a spirit of distrust and suspicion. What is the reason for this unhappy state of affairs?

² What is missing is love, the kind of love that is sincere concern for the lasting welfare of other people. And why is it missing? Getting right to the root of the problem, the Bible states: "He that does not love has not come to know God, because God is love." (1 John 4:8) Oh, it is true that there are self-seeking individuals who *profess* to believe in God, even attending church. But the fact is that they do not really *know* God. To "know" God means to be well acquainted with

---

1. (a) What has caused many people to conclude that they ought to look out for themselves and not be too concerned about other people? (b) What has been the result?
2. (a) How does the Bible identify the root of the problem? (b) What does it mean to "know" God?

his personality, to recognize his authority and then to act in harmony with it. (Jeremiah 22:16; Titus 1:16) So, then, to have the true enjoyment of life that is possible only when one freely expresses love and receives it from others, we must get to know God well and apply what we learn.

[3] "By this the love of God was made manifest in our case, because God sent forth his only-begotten Son into the world that we might gain life through him," wrote the apostle John. "The love is in this respect, not that we have [first] loved God, but that he loved us and sent forth his Son as a propitiatory sacrifice for our sins. Beloved ones, if this is how God loved us, then we are ourselves under obligation to love one another." (1 John 4:9-11) God did not hold back, letting the unloving conduct of mankind stifle his own love. As stated at Romans 5:8: "God recommends his own love to us in that, while we were yet sinners, Christ died for us."

[4] How many people are there that you love so much that you would be willing to lay down your life for them—people who have never done anything for you? If you are a parent, moved by the natural affection that makes you safeguard your child's life at the risk of your own, who is there for whom you would be willing to have your child die? That is the kind of love that God showed for us. (John 3:16) How does it make you feel toward God? If we really appreciate what he has done, we will find that it is no burden to obey his commandments.—1 John 5:3.

---

3. In what manner has God outstandingly shown his love for mankind?
4. How does that make you personally feel toward God?

⁵ On the night before his death, Jesus gave his disciples one of those commandments. It would identify them as being different from the rest of the world. He said: "I am giving you a new commandment, that you love one another." The commandment was "new" in that they were being told to love others, not merely as they loved themselves, but, Jesus said, "just as I have loved you." That would mean even being willing to lay down their lives for one another. (John 13:34, 35; 1 John 3:16) By our demonstrating this kind of love we also show our devotion to God. How is that? Because we are proving that the Devil is a liar in charging that no human will continue to obey God if his own life, his soul, is endangered. (Job 2:1-10) Obviously, obedience to this "new commandment" requires deep concern for one another. It means sparing no effort, not even our own life, to provide spiritual and material help for other servants of God where there is need. —James 1:27; 2:15, 16; 1 Thessalonians 2:8.

⁶ Loving deeds are not to be limited to fellow believers, however. Christ died for the world of mankind, not just for those who had become his disciples during his earthly ministry. Thus the Scriptures urge us: "As long as we have time favorable for it, let us work what is good toward all, but especially toward those related to us in the faith." (Galatians 6:10) There are many opportunities to do this every day of our lives. When we are not narrow, but openhearted and generous in showing love to others, we give evidence that we really are 'sons of our Father in

5. (a) What is the "new commandment" that Jesus gave to his disciples? (b) How is our devotion to God as ruler here involved? (c) What, then, are some of the things we should be doing for fellow servants of God?
6. Toward whom else is love to be shown, and why?

the heavens, because he makes his sun rise upon wicked people and good and makes it rain upon righteous people and unrighteous.'—Matthew 5:43-48.

RESPECT FOR THE PERSON AND PROPERTY OF OTHERS

[7] We live in the midst of an unloving world. You perhaps realize that you have not always been as considerate of others as you could have been. Even those who know what is right easily pick up bad habits from associates. (1 Corinthians 15:33) So, if a person is to serve God, there is need for a conscientious effort to 'make his mind over.' (Romans 12:1, 2) He needs to change his attitude toward the person and property of others.

[8] In some areas there is shocking disregard for the possessions of other people. Just for a "thrill," youths destroy both private and public property, or they deliberately deface objects that others have worked hard to acquire. Other people, who may express dismay at such vandalism, contribute to it by discarding litter in parks, on streets or in public buildings, wherever they may be. Are these loving things to do? Are they consistent with Jesus' admonition: "All things, therefore, that you want men to do to you, you also must likewise do to them"? (Matthew 7:12) Does such conduct demonstrate that one is in full accord with God's purpose for this earth to become a Paradise?

[9] Concern for one's life and possessions makes

---

7. What may easily influence how we treat the person and property of other people?
8. (a) What shows widespread disregard for the property of others? (b) What in the Bible, if applied, would hold a person back from doing such things?
9. (a) How does stealing affect the lives of everyone? (b) Why is stealing wrong in the eyes of God?

it necessary in many places to keep doors locked, or windows barred, or to have a watchdog. Stores have to raise prices to compensate for what is stolen. Stealing is common; but it has no place in the lives of those who are preparing for life in God's new order. They must learn to act in a way that contributes to the security of their fellowmen. The Bible shows that it is the "gift of God" that a man should be able to "see good for all his hard work." So it is wrong to try to deprive him of the results of his work. (Ecclesiastes 3:13; 5:18) There are many people who, in the past, were dishonest, but they have changed. Not only do they refrain from stealing; they have learned the joy of giving to others. (Acts 20:35) With a desire to please God, they have taken to heart what is written at Ephesians 4:28: "Let the stealer steal no more, but rather let him do hard work, doing with his hands what is good work, that he may have something to distribute to someone in need."

[10] Often the need of others is not for something material, but simply for kindness to them as individuals, especially when things go wrong. Yet, when one's failings or errors come to light, what often happens? It is not unusual to hear angry outbursts, screaming, abusive speech or cutting remarks. Even some who acknowledge that this is wrong fail to control their tongue. What can help a person to overcome such a habit? Basically, what is lacking is love, and that indicates there is a need to get to know God. When a person really appreciates the extent to which God has dealt mercifully with him, he will not find it so difficult

10. (a) How, by the way we speak to others, can we show consideration for them? (b) What will aid a person to learn to show love in this way?

to be forgiving to others. Moreover, in imitation of God's example, he may even begin to see ways to come to the aid of the offender, offering kind assistance with a view to improvement.—Matthew 18:21-35; Ephesians 4:31–5:2.

[11] It is true that other people may not apply this fine counsel from God's Word in their dealings with us. Despite our sincere motives, we may at times find that we are the object of their cruel abuse. What will we do then? The Bible counsels: "Do not let yourself be conquered by the evil, but keep conquering the evil with the good." (Romans 12:17-21; 1 Peter 2:21-23) Unexpected kindness on our part may actually soften their attitude and bring out their better qualities. Whatever their reaction, we can be sure that when we conform to God's way, we are giving evidence that we uphold His way of ruling, which is based on love.

OVERCOMING RACIAL, NATIONAL, SOCIAL PREJUDICE

[12] An individual who has real love is not influenced by race, skin color, nationality or social status. Why not? Because he appreciates the Bible truth that "[God] made out of one man every nation of men." (Acts 17:26) All humans are therefore related. No race is inherently superior to another.

[13] No one has any reason to boast because of his ancestry, race, color, nationality or station in life. "All have sinned and fall short of the glory of God." (Romans 3:23) To attain righteousness,

11. Why should we not be abusive in our speech even when others are unkind to us?
12, 13. How does the Bible help a person to eliminate any feelings of racial, national or social prejudice?

all must depend on the ransom sacrifice of Christ. And the Bible shows that those who do so, and will be spared through the coming "great tribulation," are taken from "all nations and tribes and peoples and tongues."—Revelation 7:9, 14-17.

[14] Attempting to justify his prejudice, a man may call to mind a bad experience that he had with someone of a certain race or nationality. But it is well to remind ourselves that not everyone of that race or nationality was involved in the wrongdoing. Furthermore, people of one's own race or nationality have no doubt been guilty of the very same things. If we hope to live in God's peaceful new order, we need to clean out of our hearts any pride that tends to alienate us from other people.

[15] What is in our hearts is sooner or later manifest in our speech. As Christ Jesus said: "Out of the heart's abundance [the] mouth speaks." (Luke 6:45) What if speech reflecting prejudice toward people of another race or nationality were to stumble someone who was showing interest in God's provision for salvation? This could lead to serious consequences for the one who spoke unlovingly. Christ Jesus warned: "Whoever stumbles one of these little ones that believe, it would be finer for him if a millstone such as is turned by an ass were put around his neck and he were actually pitched into the sea." —Mark 9:42.

[16] Without regard to race, nationality or station

14. Why is a bad personal experience not a valid basis for hard feelings against people of a certain race or nationality?
15. If a person's comments about race or nationality were to stumble a fellow believer, how would this affect his own standing before God and Christ?
16. How did Jesus indicate the impartiality with which we should show that we care about other people?

in life, a Christian is under obligation to take an interest in others. (James 2:1-9) Jesus well expressed the point when he said: "When you spread a feast, invite poor people, crippled, lame, blind; and you will be happy, because they have nothing with which to repay you." (Luke 14:13, 14) When we thus show that we deeply care about other people, we give evidence that we are truly reflecting the qualities of God.

LOVING CONCERN
FOR THE ETERNAL WELFARE OF OTHERS

[17] Our concern for others, of course, should not be limited to their present physical needs. Nor would our love be complete simply because we were kindly in our dealings with people of all races, nationalities and positions in life. For life to have real meaning, these persons need knowledge of Jehovah God and his purposes. In prayer to his Father, Jesus Christ said: "This means everlasting life, their taking in knowledge of you, the only true God, and of the one whom you sent forth, Jesus Christ." (John 17:3) If you have read this book from the beginning, you know how to lay hold of that prize. You have seen for yourself what the Scriptures say about the foretold "great tribulation," and the physical evidences that confirm its nearness. You know that God's kingdom is the only hope for mankind. Others, too, need this vital knowledge. Does love for Jehovah and for your fellowman move you to want to share it with them?

[18] When speaking of the "conclusion of the

17. (a) What is the most valuable thing that we can share with others? (b) Why should we feel moved to do so?
18. (a) At Matthew 24:14, what work did Jesus foretell for our day? (b) How should we view participation in it?

system of things," Jesus foretold: "This good news of the kingdom will be preached in all the inhabited earth for a witness to all the nations; and then the end will come." (Matthew 24:14) What a privilege to represent the Sovereign Ruler of the universe, Jehovah himself, as one of his witnesses! Opportunity to share in this special work foretold by God's Son is still open, but not for much longer.

¹⁹ In thinking about the prospect of sharing in this work as one of Jehovah's Christian witnesses, it is good to realize that it is not one's personal speaking ability, but God who opens the hearts of those who listen favorably to the good news. (Acts 16:14) If you are moved by a willing heart, Jehovah can use you to accomplish his will. The message is his and he is the one who causes it to produce results. (1 Corinthians 3:6) Consider what the apostle Paul said in his own case: "Now through the Christ we have this sort of confidence toward God. Not that we of ourselves are adequately qualified to reckon anything as issuing from ourselves, but our being adequately qualified issues from God."—2 Corinthians 3:4-6.

²⁰ We should not expect, of course, that everyone will respond favorably to the good news. Many will be indifferent; some will oppose. Yet they can change. Saul of Tarsus, who was once a persecutor of Christians, became a zealous apostle of Jesus Christ. (1 Timothy 1:12, 13) Whether others know it or not, they need the Kingdom message; so we should present it earnestly. There

19. Why should we not allow any feeling of lack in personal ability to hold us back from sharing in this work?
20. (a) Will everyone respond favorably to the good news? (b) What good is accomplished by preaching to people who are indifferent or even opposed?

is need for deep concern about their welfare, not just our own. Such concern calls for wholehearted effort in their behalf, a willingness to expend ourselves to further their lasting welfare. (1 Thessalonians 2:7, 8) Even if they do not want the Kingdom message, good is accomplished. The witness is given; Jehovah's name is magnified; a 'separating' of the people is being done.—Matthew 25:31-33.

CARING WHAT HAPPENS TO YOUR OWN FAMILY

[21] The effort that you put forth to aid others to benefit from Jehovah's loving provisions, however, should not be directed only to those outside your own family. A family head, for example, has a primary responsibility toward his own household. Their spiritual growth is directly influenced by the regularity with which he arranges for the family to discuss and study God's Word together. And when a father's prayers on behalf of the family show depth of devotion and gratitude, this can mold the attitude of the entire household.

[22] His responsibility also includes the administering of discipline. When problems arise, it may seem easier to ignore them. But if discipline is administered only when the father becomes irritated, or if problems are handled only when they become serious, something is missing. Says Proverbs 13:24: 'The father who *loves* his son is he that does look for him with discipline.' It truly is a loving father who, even when he is tired at the end of the day, is consistent in administering discipline. It is a further evidence of

---

21. What responsibility does a family head have as to the spiritual well-being of his own household?
22. Why is it important for a father to discipline his children, and what should motivate him in doing so?

love if he patiently explains things to his children
and if he takes into consideration the mental,
emotional and physical limitations of each one.
(Ephesians 6:4; Colossians 3:21) If you are a
father, do you have that kind of love for your
children? Willingness to shoulder this responsibility shows that one has an eye, not merely on
the present, but also on the future welfare of
one's family.—Proverbs 23:13, 14; 29:17.

²³ By cooperating with her husband in caring
for the spiritual condition of the family, the
wife, too, makes a major contribution to their
welfare. When she cares deeply about the children
and makes good use of her time to mold their
lives in a godly way, this usually is reflected in
their conduct and in their attitude toward her.
(Proverbs 29:15) Even in those cases where there
is no father in the home, careful teaching from
the Bible coupled with a fine example yields good
results.

²⁴ But what if a father who is in the home does
not accept God's Word? He may even subject
his wife to persecution. What should she do? If
she loves Jehovah, she certainly will not turn
her back on God. It is Satan who charged that
humans would forsake God if subjected to personal hardship, and she certainly does not want
to find herself doing Satan's bidding. (Job 2:1-5;
Proverbs 27:11) At the same time, the Bible
urges her to care deeply enough about her husband to seek his lasting welfare. Forsaking what
she knows to be the truth would not show such

23. How can a mother show that she is keenly interested in the
spiritual welfare of her family?
24. (a) If faced with opposition from one's marriage mate, what
issue should the believer keep in focus? (b) Under such circumstances, how would real love be shown for the unbelieving mate?

love; the result would no doubt be loss of eternal life for both of them. But if she remains firm in her faith, she may aid him to gain salvation. (1 Corinthians 7:10-16; 1 Peter 3:1, 2) Furthermore, by continuing to honor her marriage vows, even under difficulty, she shows her deep respect for the Author of marriage, Jehovah God.

²⁵ There is another powerful reason for a believing parent to maintain faithfulness to God even though faced with opposition. That is the children. God views with favor the young children of his devoted servants and gives assurance that these children, if obedient, will be preserved through the coming "great tribulation." Even if only one parent is a servant of Jehovah, God considerately counts such young children as "holy." (1 Corinthians 7:14) But what if the parent were to "beg off" from doing the will of God? Such parent would thereby give up, not only for himself or herself, but also for the young children, an approved standing before God. (Hebrews 12:25) What a tragic loss that would be!

²⁶ No matter what aspect of life we view, then, it is evident that there is need for us to consider, not just ourselves, but others too. We ourselves will receive love if we make it a practice to act with unselfish concern for others. (Luke 6:38) But to demonstrate genuine love and not to be misled by shortsighted human reasoning, we need to come to know Jehovah God and to enjoy a fine relationship with him. Our doing so, however, involves a choice that we must personally make.

---

25. How does the decision of the parent affect the life prospects of children?
26. To act with real benefit to ourselves and others, what do we need?

CHAPTER 16

The Choice Assuring Life in True Peace and Security

WHAT a blessing it is to have a real purpose in living, to know where you are going! And how comforting to have the certainty that there is no better, wiser course you could possibly take! What peace of mind and heart this brings! Such peace and confidence can be yours, but only if you make the right choice now in this time of opportunity.

² All the evidence shows that we cannot look to this world as the source of true peace and security. The Bible points us, therefore, not to the world, not even to ourselves, but to Jehovah God as the one Source of true peace and security. By our coming to know him and his purposes for mankind we come to understand why we are here on earth and why things are as they are today. We learn of the great issue facing all mankind and how this issue, involving Jehovah's universal sovereignty, affects each of us and our hope of life. By the light of God's Word we can see the root causes of mankind's problems. We can learn to weigh the rightness and wisdom of our goals and gain a stable, reliable set of moral standards by which to live. Yes, even when faced with sickness, old age or death, we can have the comforting assurance that, by doing Jehovah's will, we have

1. If we make the right choice, what peace and confidence can be ours now?
2. How does our coming to know Jehovah and his purposes affect our entire outlook on life?

the guarantee of life in a righteous, healthful new order, even, if necessary, by a resurrection from the dead.

³ No wonder, then, that Isaiah 26:4 exhorts: "Trust in Jehovah, you people, for all times, for in Jah Jehovah is the Rock of times indefinite." Unchanging, almighty and eternal, Jehovah is indeed the one on whom to rest all our hopes. Do you want to qualify to enjoy his guidance and protection, not just for the present, but for all future time in his promised new order? What must you do?

⁴ Mankind as a whole has been alienated from God because of the sin of our first parents. To gain Jehovah's favor, all persons need to become reconciled to him, to enter into a favorable relationship with him. God has opened the way for every person to do so by means of his Son and his Son's sacrifice on behalf of the world. (2 Corinthians 5:19-21; Ephesians 2:12, 13) Yet, it is not enough for us now simply to *say* we want God's friendship.

⁵ We should be willing, even eager, to *prove* to him that we want this and want it out of a right motive. Jehovah God would certainly not be pleased if we sought his friendship only as a means of escaping some disaster. While there is a genuine urgency in our day due to the nearness of God's judgment, our seeking a right standing with him cannot be just for a certain period, nor just to survive the coming "great tribulation." It must be for all time to come. Only genuine love will give us this motivation. So that we may

3. Why is Jehovah the one on whom to rest all our hopes?
4. To gain Jehovah's favor, what do we need, and what makes it possible?
5. What should be our motivation in seeking Jehovah's friendship?

demonstrate the sincerity of our desire, Jehovah God has set out in his Word certain things we each must do to gain reconciliation with him.

A LIVING FAITH

⁶ Jehovah is a God of truth. We can, and rightly should, have absolute confidence in his promises. In fact, "without faith it is impossible to please him well, for he that approaches God must believe that he is and that he becomes the rewarder of those earnestly seeking him." (Hebrews 11:6) Do you have such faith? If you do, then you will be confident that everything that God does has a good and righteous purpose, and that he always has our best interests at heart. From his creative works and, far more so, from his written Word, you can see that he is not only all-wise and all-powerful but also a God of loving-kindness. He will, of course, never turn aside from his righteous standards or abandon his purposes. Yet, even though we are imperfect and commit errors, what he does will result in blessings for us if we love righteousness. We need to be convinced of this if we are to have a faith that will give us strength and comfort under all circumstances.

⁷ Then, even when we receive correction, reproof or discipline, we will know that it is for our good and our eternal welfare. We thus come to trust Jehovah God as a son or daughter trusts a loving, wise and strong father. (Psalm 103:13, 14 [102:13, 14, *Dy*]; Proverbs 3:11, 12) Having such faith, we will not question or doubt his wise counsel, nor the rightness of his ways, even though for a time we may not entirely understand

6. To please God, what confidence must we have regarding him?
7. How will confidence in Jehovah's rightness and wisdom safeguard us?

certain matters. This will be a safeguard to us. We thereby place ourselves among those the psalmist describes, saying: "Abundant peace belongs to those loving your law, and for them there is no stumbling block."—Psalm 119:165 [118:165, *Dy*]; Proverbs 3:5-8.

[8] But "faith apart from works is inactive," it is "dead," as James 2:20, 26 points out. Genuine faith moves a person to action. What is one of the first things true faith moves a person to do? It causes him to act in the way the apostle Peter exhorted persons in his day to do, saying: "Repent . . . and turn around so as to get your sins blotted out, that seasons of refreshing may come from the person of Jehovah." (Acts 3:19) What does this mean?

REPENTING AND TURNING AROUND

[9] In the Bible, repentance denotes a change—a change of mind accompanied by regret or remorse for a former course or for bad acts committed. (2 Corinthians 7:9-11) If we are going to enjoy the promised "seasons of refreshing" from God, we cannot just repent over one or more wrong acts of the past. Instead, we must show repentance because we recognize that as a result of our being offspring of Adam our very *nature* is sinful. As the apostle John states: "If we make the statement: 'We have no sin,' we are misleading ourselves . . . we are making [God] a liar, and his word is not in us." (1 John 1:8, 10) We should properly represent our Creator, serving in 'his image and likeness.' Yet inherited sin keeps

---

8. (a) Why is faith alone not enough? (b) To what action mentioned at Acts 3:19 should faith move us?
9. (a) What is true repentance? (b) Over what do we need to repent?

us from doing this in a perfect way; we 'miss the mark,' which is what the word "sin" as used in the Bible literally means.—Genesis 1:26; Romans 3:23.

¹⁰ So we are 'debtors' to God and need his forgiveness. (Matthew 6:12) We realize that we owe our life to him as our Creator. But now we also learn that, through his Son's sacrifice of his perfect human life, all mankind was purchased or ransomed—and that includes us. Having been "bought with a price" of such great value, we should not be the "slaves of men," not even of ourselves and our own selfish desires. (1 Corinthians 7:23) Yet, before our learning and accepting the truth, is that not what all of us were? —John 8:31-34.

¹¹ Do you appreciate God's gift of his Son, and do you appreciate in your heart what God has done in opening the way for escape from bondage to sin and death? Then surely you will sincerely regret any past failure to use your life in obedience to your Creator. This will move you to heartfelt repentance over having followed a life course like that of the world, out of harmony with God's will and purposes.—Acts 17:28, 30; Revelation 4:11.

¹² This true repentance leads to a 'turning around,' which is what the word "conversion" means. The genuinely repentant person does not merely regret his past misuse of his life; he *rejects* that wrong course and actually comes to hate his wrong ways. He shows this by 'turning around' and doing God's will, bringing his life

10, 11. (a) To whom are we indebted for life, and why? (b) So, how should we be using our lives?
12. How does a repentant person show that he really has rejected his former course?

into harmony with God's purposes. [...] "works that befit repentance."—Acts [...] mans 6:11.

[13] Part of this repenting and turning [...] cludes doing what Jesus Christ said [...] must do, namely, 'disowning ourselves.' (Matthew 16:24) That is, we no longer lay any selfish claim to ourselves or to any supposed 'right' to live our lives according to just our own selfish desires with no concern for God's will and purposes. Instead, we recognize that Jehovah God actually has full claim to our lives, not only because he is the Creator but more especially because of his Son's purchase of the whole human race through his ransom sacrifice. As the apostle Paul expresses it, we 'do not belong to ourselves, for we were bought with a price.' (1 Corinthians 6:19, 20) So, we do not misuse the grand freedom that the truth opens up for us, but instead we submit ourselves fully to do God's will as directed by his Son. (Galatians 5:13; 1 Peter 2:16) And we do this, not only because it is right, but because we love Jehovah God with 'all our heart, soul, mind and strength.' (Mark 12:29, 30) Surely this calls for each of us to live a life of full dedication or devotion to God. Is this course burdensome or oppressive? To the contrary, it enables one to enjoy life as never before.—Matthew 11:28-30.

MAKING PUBLIC DECLARATION FOR SALVATION

[14] It is a fine thing to make expression to God

---

13. (a) What is the meaning of Jesus' statement that those who want to follow him must 'disown themselves'? (b) For what reason do we thus fully submit ourselves to Jehovah, and how does it affect our lives?
14. (a) When a person comes to the point that he feels moved to acknowledge Jehovah's rightful ownership of him, how can he make expression of this to God? (b) What else should he desire to do, as indicated at Romans 10:10, 13?

ayer of our faith in his provisions, acknowl-
ging his rightful ownership of us. But there is
still more that we can and should want to do.
Romans 10:10, 13 tells us: "With the heart one
exercises faith for righteousness, but with the
mouth one makes public declaration for salvation,"
and "everyone who calls on the name of Jehovah
will be saved." We should therefore be glad to
make public expression of our faith in Jehovah
God and in his provisions, doing so from a heart
full of appreciation. One way in which we are to
do this is in connection with water baptism.

¹⁵ When Jesus Christ began his public ministry
among the world of mankind, he presented himself to John the Baptist to be immersed in water.
The Bible describes him as then saying to God:
"I am come to do your will." (Hebrews 10:9;
Psalm 40:7, 8 [39:8, 9, *Dy*]) Jesus instructed that
all those coming to be his disciples should also be
baptized. Are you ready for water baptism as
evidence that you are such a disciple?—Matthew
28:19, 20.

¹⁶ It is a grand privilege to become a dedicated,
baptized witness of Jehovah, the only true God,
the rightful Sovereign of all the universe. Review
now what this involves: Jehovah has lovingly
opened the way for you to come into an approved
relationship with him. But to do that you must
have faith. You must really believe that the Bible
is the inspired Word of God. (2 Timothy 3:16, 17)
You must exercise faith in Christ Jesus as the
only means by which you can gain an acceptable
standing with God. (Acts 4:12) You need to

15. Why should we think seriously about water baptism?
16. (a) How can you determine whether you are ready to get
baptized? (b) What does the presiding overseer do by way of
aiding individuals in their preparation for baptism?

appreciate your complete dependence on Jehovah God and earnestly desire to submit your entire life to him to do his will, not just for a few years, but forever. Is that truly what is in your heart? As you now know, this involves being "no part of the world." (John 17:16; 1 John 2:15) As evidence that you have repented and 'turned around,' you must have abandoned the practices that are contrary to God's righteous standards and now be sincerely endeavoring to do the things that God commands. Have you, because of heartfelt love for Jehovah, made your mind over so that this is now the way you view life? (Romans 12:1, 2) Then, the Bible encourages you to make "public declaration" of such faith. If this is your desire, it would be appropriate to approach the presiding overseer of the congregation of Jehovah's Christian witnesses in your area and openly make known how you feel. He will arrange for a review with you of the basic teachings of the Bible in preparation for baptism.

[17] The Scriptures associate baptism with salvation, and appropriately so. The apostle Peter, after referring to the salvation of Noah and his family through the global flood, says: "That which corresponds to this is also now saving you, namely, baptism, (not the putting away of the filth of the flesh, but the request made to God for a good conscience,) through the resurrection of Jesus Christ." (1 Peter 3:21) How is this? It is not the baptismal water in itself that does anything for those baptized. But the ones presenting themselves for water immersion want God's forgiveness of their sins so that they may have a clean conscience toward him. They know that

17. In what way is baptism definitely involved in gaining salvation?

such forgiveness is possible by faith in the value of Christ Jesus' shed blood. On the basis of such faith, they request forgiveness from God and make this evident by presenting themselves for baptism. (Acts 2:38) God grants them the requested good conscience. Thus the individual is delivered or saved from the present wicked system of things and enjoys the grand prospects that belong to those who do the will of God. (Galatians 1:3, 4; 1 John 2:17) Thus, Christian water baptism is vital to those who desire life in God's righteous new order, now near at hand.

[18] When you take this step, that will not, of course, mark the end of your making 'public declaration of your faith.' To continue to have Jehovah's approval, you must never cease calling upon Jehovah and looking to him for guidance. This needs to be done, not just in the privacy of your own home, but publicly. This includes sharing zealously in the special work that Christ Jesus gives to all those submitting to his headship. That work is preaching the good news of God's kingdom in all the world and making disciples of people of all the nations.—Matthew 24:14; 28:19.

CHERISHING YOUR RELATIONSHIP WITH GOD

[19] Now, then, how can you ensure that, once gained, your relationship with God will be an *enduring* one, one that will assure you, not just survival through the coming world destruction, but an eternity of service to Jehovah in joyful peace and security?

[20] For one thing you will want to keep growing in knowledge of him. Personal study of his Word

---

18. Using the Bible, show how we must continue to make 'public declaration of our faith.'
19, 20. How important is personal study in ensuring that one's relationship with Jehovah will endure?

will aid you greatly in this, and even more so will application to your daily life of the things learned. You can find real pleasure in acquiring the treasures of knowledge, understanding and wisdom that God has stored up in his Word the Bible. You can be like the one that Psalm 1:2, 3 describes: "His delight is in the law of Jehovah, and in his law he reads in an undertone day and night. And he will certainly become like a tree planted by streams of water, that gives its own fruit in its season and the foliage of which does not wither, and everything he does will succeed." Yes, if you develop a real love for the truth and for knowledge of God, this will cause you to walk in "ways of pleasantness" and in 'roadways of peace,' because it will give you the wisdom to face all life's problems. (Proverbs 3:13, 17, 18) Your thirst for knowledge, evidenced by your real interest in Bible study, will show that you are preparing for life in the new order, when "the earth will certainly be filled with the knowledge of Jehovah as the waters are covering the very sea."—Isaiah 11:9.

²¹ Something else that you vitally need if you are to "hold fast the public declaration of our hope without wavering" is to congregate with others who are devoted servants of Jehovah. By regularly attending the meetings of Jehovah's people you will find genuine incitement to love and fine works, encouragement to continue maintaining your right relationship with God. (Hebrews 10:23-25) You will find strengthening evidence in such pleasant, family-like association that the peacefulness and security promised for God's new order are a reality.—Psalm 133:1 [132:1, *Dy*]; 1 Corinthians 14:26, 33.

21. Why is regular meeting attendance a necessity in the life of Jehovah's people?

²² In the congregation you can benefit from another loving provision. Himself the 'Fine Shepherd,' Jesus Christ has 'undershepherds' on earth, spiritually older men or "elders" who are to care for his "sheep." This is a powerful factor even now in the enjoyment of peace and security among God's congregated people throughout the earth. (1 Peter 5:2, 3) These men "prove to be like a hiding place from the wind and a place of concealment from the rainstorm, like streams of water in a waterless country, like the shadow of a heavy crag in an exhausted land." (Isaiah 32:1, 2) Yes, in stormy times of trouble, of pressure and stress due to worldly opposition or personal difficulties, by their rocklike faith and their firm adherence to God's Word these spiritually older men or "elders" can give real support. They can supply you with refreshing counsel, help and encouragement.

²³ True, human imperfections will manifest themselves, even among God's servants. We all make mistakes daily. (James 3:2) But will we let ourselves be stumbled by the imperfections of others and let their imperfections somehow mar our relationship with Jehovah God? Since we, too, err and say and do things we later regret, should we not show others the same mercy and forgiveness we want for ourselves? (Matthew 6:14, 15) If we are to prove ourselves fit subjects for life in God's peaceful new order, we must now demonstrate our ability to get along with others in peace. We cannot love God without

22. How can the "elders" in the congregation aid us in times of opposition and personal difficulty?
23. What will prevent us from ever allowing the imperfections of others to mar our relationship with Jehovah?

loving also our brother for whom Christ died.
—1 John 4:20, 21.

[24] Your right relationship with God gives you
another grand privilege: the approach to God
by prayer with the assurance that he hears you.
Cherish that privilege and use it daily, throughout
the day. Problems will arise; your own imperfections may trouble you. Yet the Bible counsels: "Do not be anxious over anything, but in
everything by prayer and supplication along with
thanksgiving let your petitions be made known to
God; and the peace of God that excels all thought
will guard your hearts and your mental powers
by means of Christ Jesus."—Philippians 4:6, 7.

[25] By choosing to serve Jehovah God, the true
Source of peace and security, and placing your
hope in his righteous new order, you have made
a right start. Now, as the apostle expresses it,
"you have need of endurance, in order that, after
you have done the will of God, you may receive
the fulfillment of the promise." (Hebrews 10:36)
Having tasted the blessings of a right relationship
with Jehovah God, determine never to give it up.
Never let the fleeting pleasures of the world draw
you away. Though trials and persecutions from
an enemy world become severe, remember that
they, too, are but temporary. Compared with the
blessings that Jehovah God will grant to those
loving him, such sufferings are as nothing.—2 Corinthians 4:16-18.

[26] Continue in the course of godly devotion,
confident that it is the best way of life now and

24. What place should prayer have in our lives?
25. When faced with trials and persecution for our faith, what will help us to endure?
26. (a) In what do we today especially have reason to rejoice? (b) Like the psalmist, how should we always feel about Jehovah and our relationship with him?

that it will lead unfailingly to eternal life in God's new order. (1 Timothy 4:8) Rejoice in the evidence of the nearness of that new order and the everlasting peace and security that it will bring. As you keep building your relationship with Jehovah God, may you always feel as did the inspired psalmist who wrote:

"God is the rock of my heart and my share to time indefinite. For, look! the very ones keeping away from you will perish. You will certainly silence every one immorally leaving you. But as for me, the drawing near to God is good for me. In the Sovereign Lord Jehovah I have placed my refuge, to declare all your works."—Psalm 73:26-28 [72:26-28, *Dy*].

∞∞∞∞∞∞∞∞∞∞∞∞∞∞∞∞∞∞∞∞∞∞∞∞

REFERENCES

1. New York *Times,* January 21, 1973, p. 32 B.   2. Special to the Washington *Post,* published in *The State Journal,* Lansing —East Lansing, Michigan, July 22, 1970, p. 1.   3. *World War I* (1962), by Hanson W. Baldwin, p. 1.   4. *The Environmental Crisis* (1970), edited by Harold W. Helfrich, Jr., p. 84. 5. Trenton, New Jersey, *Times-Advertiser,* June 13, 1971, p. 16. 6. *Population and Food* (1971), edited by R. S. Leisner and E. J. Kormondy, p. 18; also *Readings in Human Population Ecology* (1971), chapter on "Prevalence of People," by R. O. Greep, p. 21. 7. Atlanta *Journal,* December 10, 1971.   8. *U.S. News & World Report,* May 1, 1967, p. 64.   9. *Time,* February 2, 1970, pp. 62, 63.   10. *The Australian,* November 3, 1971.   11. New York *Times,* June 10, 1971.   12. *Wall Street Journal,* April 14, 1970.   13. New York *Times,* April 4, 1972.   14. New York *Times,* June 6, 1971, Sec. 4, p. 14.   15. *World Book Encyclopedia* (1970 ed.), Vol. 16, p. 207.   16. New York *Times,* December 29, 1966, p. 3.   17. *La Dernière Heure,* January 7, 1967.   18. Pittsburgh, Pa., *Courier,* November 9, 1935. 19. *Encyclopædia Britannica* (1959), Vol. 15, p. 387.   20. *Science* (Vol. 178, No. 4062), November 17, 1972, p. 725.   21. *New Catholic Encyclopedia* (1967), Vol. 2, p. 384.   22. *Broadman Bible Commentary,* Vol. 1, pp. 117, 198.   23. New York *Times,* Book Review, June 28, 1959.   24. *The Age,* Melbourne, Australia, December 9, 1967.   25. *Schweizergeschichte vom Dreiländerbund bis zum Völkerbund,* 11th unchanged edition, 1953, p. 198.   26. *World Book Encyclopedia* (1970), Vol. 20, p. 379. 27. *Wall Street Journal,* August 15, 1972.   28. London *Star,* August 4, 1960.   29. New York *Post,* March 14, 1969, page 2 of magazine section.   30. New York *Times,* March 25, 1969. 31. New York *Times,* May 11, 1972.   32. *Science Year,* The World Book Science Annual, p. 320.   33. New York *Times Magazine,* October 9, 1966, p. 146.   34. *Encore,* Autumn 1960, p. 31.   35. Jacksonville, Florida, *Journal,* May 18, 1966. 36. *Theological Dictionary of the New Testament* (1959), edited by G. Friedrich, p. 587.   37. *Encyclopædia Britannica* (1959), Vol. 7, p. 110.   38. New York *Times,* January 25, 1971, p. 42.

Can You Prove that the Bible Is Really God's Word?

Millions of persons need to have their questions answered if they are going to accept the Bible as being the word of God. For example, they want to know:

- Is the Genesis account of creation fact or fiction?
- Was there an earth-wide flood?
- Can you expect secular history always to agree with the Bible?
- Are the miracles of the Bible true?
- Does the Bible contradict itself?
- Is the Bible practical for our day?

Equip yourself with many convincing proofs of the Bible's divine origin. Then you can help others. Obtain the 192-page book **Is the Bible Really the Word of God?**

Also available is the illustrated and documented 192-page book **Did Man Get Here by Evolution or by Creation?**

To obtain your copy of either of these attractive hardbound books postpaid, just send 25c, or 50c for both.

Write to **Watchtower**, using an address from the next page.

OTHER BIBLE TEACHINGS MADE CLEAR

Would you like to know what the Bible really teaches about many other subjects? Then obtain the pocket-size book **The Truth That Leads to Eternal Life**. This hard-covered, 192-page Bible study aid will be sent to you postpaid for just 25c. It will tell you:

- ✔ Where the dead are.
- ✔ How you can identify the true religion.
- ✔ What the Bible says about popular customs.
- ✔ How wicked spirits mislead mankind.
- ✔ What to do to build a happy family life.

Do you have a sincere desire to know what God has to say on these matters? Jehovah's witnesses will be happy to give you further help. How? By a free, one-hour-a-week discussion of the Bible in your home, for six months.

If you would like to have someone come to your home to discuss Bible questions with you, write to **Watchtower** at an address given below.

ALASKA 99507: 2552 East 48th Ave., Anchorage. AUSTRALIA: 11 Beresford Road, Strathfield, N.S.W. 2135. BAHAMAS: Box N-1247, Nassau, N.P. BARBADOS, W.I.: Fontabelle Rd., Bridgetown. BRAZIL: Rua Guaíra, 216, Bosque da Saúde, 04142 São Paulo, SP. BRITISH HONDURAS: Box 257, Belize. CANADA: 150 Bridgeland Ave., Toronto, Ont. M6A 1Z5. CONGO REPUBLIC: B.P. 2.114, Brazzaville. ENGLAND: Watch Tower House, The Ridgeway, London NW7 1RN. FIJI: Box 23, Suva. FRANCE: 81 rue du Point-du-Jour, 92100 Boulogne-Billancourt. GERMANY (WESTERN): Postfach 13025, 62 Wiesbaden-Dotzheim. GHANA: Box 760, Accra. GUYANA: 50 Brickdam, Georgetown 16. HAWAII 96814: 1228 Pensacola St., Honolulu. HONG KONG: 312 Prince Edward Rd., Second Floor, Kowloon. INDIA: South Avenue, Santa Cruz, Bombay 400054. INDONESIA: Jl Batuceper 47, Jakarta, DKI. IRELAND: 86 Lindsay Rd., Glasnevin, Dublin 9. JAMAICA, W.I.: 41 Trafalgar Rd., Kingston 10. KENYA: Box 47788, Nairobi. LEEWARD ISLANDS, W.I.: Box 119, St. Johns, Antigua. LIBERIA: P.O. Box 171, Monrovia. MALAYSIA: 20 Scotland Close, Penang. NEWFOUNDLAND, CANADA: 239 Pennywell Rd., St. John's. NEW ZEALAND: 621 New North Rd., Auckland 3. NIGERIA: P.O. Box 194, Yaba, Lagos State. PAKISTAN: 8-E Habibullah Rd., Lahore 3. PANAMA: Apartado 1386, Panama 1. PAPUA: Box 113, Port Moresby. PHILIPPINE REPUBLIC: 186 Roosevelt Ave., San Francisco del Monte, Quezon City D-503. RHODESIA: P.O. Box 1462, Salisbury. SIERRA LEONE: Box 136, Freetown. SOUTH AFRICA: Private Bag 2, P.O. Elandsfontein, Transvaal. SRI LANKA, REP. OF: 62 Layard's Road, Colombo 5. SWITZERLAND: Ulmenweg 45, P.O. Box 477, CH-3601 Thun. TRINIDAD, W.I.: 2 La Seiva Road, Maraval, Port of Spain. UNITED STATES OF AMERICA: 117 Adams St., Brooklyn, N.Y. 11201.